C000245704

The Boulevard
voices

The great Billy Batten with the Northern Union Challenge Cup that he helped Hull to win for the first time in 1914.

Tempus ORAL HISTORY *Series*

The Boulevard
voices

Compiled by
Raymond Fletcher

TEMPUS

First published 2001
Copyright © Raymond Fletcher, 2001

Tempus Publishing Limited
The Mill, Brimscombe Port,
Stroud, Gloucestershire, GL5 2QG

ISBN 0 7524 2190 5

Typesetting and origination by
Tempus Publishing Limited
Printed in Great Britain by
Midway Colour Print, Wiltshire

Hull captain Greg Mackey lifts the Premiership Trophy after the shock defeat of Widnes in 1991. Lee Jackson is also triumphant.

Contents

Introduction

Hull FC loomed large in my formative years. I went to Chiltern Street School, whose tower soared over the famous Threepenny Stand, and later attended Riley High School in Boulevard, passing Airlie Street (which provided the 'Airlie Birds' nickname) on the way. I started going to The Boulevard when I was about five or six. At first it was just to play at Cowboys and Indians on Bunker's Hill with my friends. We'd go to the match at half-time, because they opened the gates then and we got in for free. We'd just lark about at the top and at the back of Bunker's Hill, at the Gordon Street end where it was all overgrown with weeds and long grass. Then I suppose I heard the crowd cheering and stopped to watch what was happening on the field. It must have been good, because gradually I stopped playing and watched more of the rugby, and have been doing so ever since.

My interest in Hull, and rugby league generally, was then generated by my dad. Other kids might have been read fairy tales by their parents, but I would listen for hours to my dad telling me all about the great Hull teams he had seen. They were mostly about the side that won the Cup in 1914. In fact, even now I could probably run through the names of that team more quickly than I could the present one. Let's see: Ned Rogers, Alf Francis, Billy Batten, Bert Gilbert, Jack Harrison and so on. Even my mam, who only ever went to one match, knew a lot about the team, and she would tell me about Hessle Road characters who would pretend to be players. One would be Jimmy Devereux, sidestepping the lamp posts. And decades later she would still say when she saw a bouncing baby boy, 'He's got legs like Billy Batten'.

Having moved to the Leeds area over thirty years ago, I am no longer a fanatical supporter of Hull. I like to think I became more and more neutral during my many years as the *Yorkshire Post* rugby league correspondent, but there is still a strong pang of nostalgia for the Airlie Birds, and I retain the dream of Hull winning at Wembley. How I empathise with the fans' stories recalled in the *Wembley Heartbreak* chapter.

Compiling this book, then, has obviously been a labour of love. There are worse jobs than sitting in a pub listening to a Hull fan recalling stories about his beloved team. And the four-hour car trip to Twickenham to see England's World Cup game against Australia whizzed by in the company of Trevor Gibbons, whose non-stop reminiscing was so engrossing that we almost missed the motorway turn-off! All of the fans I interviewed spoke with such passion about *their* team, and almost everyone answered the opening question of 'Why did you start watching Hull?' with 'Because my dad took me'. The family link is still more important than any number of gimmicks; tradition also came through as a very strong tie. Even the younger fans spoke with pride and passion about Hull's distinctive, irregular, black and white hooped strip. I am with them on this matter. It is Hull. There is no wish to halt progress, but change for change's sake improves nothing.

While looking to the future, Hull fans can look back with pride as supporters of the oldest club in the game, Huddersfield's claims for that distinction being debatable. Formed in 1865 by a group of former public schoolboys, Hull FC became founder members of the Northern Union in 1895, following the breakaway from the English Rugby Union, which eventually led to the new game of rugby league. Since then the club and the city have been acknowledged as one of rugby league's major strongholds and its supporters among the most fanatical in the land.

Unfortunately, a small minority of hooligans has long besmirched the club's good name, and they dragged it into the mud with an invasion of the pitch after their semi-final defeat by Leeds Rhinos at Huddersfield's Alfred McAlpine Stadium just as I was beginning to compile this book. There was a serious threat of Hull FC being suspended, but the genuine fans rallied round and their attitude helped to save the club. They signed a fans' charter, pledging good behaviour and a promise to make The Boulevard a welcoming place for all visiting supporters. It is those sort of fans who have contributed to this book and whose stories confirm what an important and proud part Hull FC play in the community of the city.

Raymond Fletcher
January 2001

Acknowledgements

My first thanks must go to the many Hull fans who were willing and eager to regale me with their stories of the club they feel so passionately about. I was so totally engrossed in listening to them that we frequently went beyond the time allotted. I only wish I could have printed every word, and apologise if editorial restrictions have meant cutting anyone's favourite memory.

I am particularly indebted to the *Yorkshire Post* for the use of several photographs and facsimiles of reports. The paper also provided me with twenty years of immense satisfaction, as its rugby league correspondent, and I will always be grateful for that. They actually paid me to watch Hull!

The *Hull Daily Mail* also gave permission for the reproduction of photographs, cartoons and reports. I thank them for that and for the many reports and articles which make up much-treasured scrapbooks of the 1950s and '60s which I still have.

I am uncertain of the origins of some of the photographs used in this book, but I am sure they have been supplied over the years by photographer friends such as Andrew Varley and Andrew Howard, plus the staff at *Rugby Leaguer* and *League Express*. My thanks to all of them, and to a few others who have provided help and information, however small.

On a personal note, I would like to remember my late father, whose stories of the club and its great players enchanted me and have stayed with me forever. My Leeds-born wife must also take some credit, or blame, for allowing me to retain my roots. Her honeymoon present to me was a black and white scarf!

Raymond Fletcher

Sir Tom Courtenay's contribution is extracted by kind permission from *Dear Tom* by Tom Courtenay, published in 2000 by Doubleday, a division of Transworld Publishers. All rights reserved.

Programme for 5 January 1952.

CHAPTER 1
Earliest Memories

Hull fans display a variety of headgear as they pack the Threepenny Stand in the 1920s.

Bob Taylor, a great Hull forward of the 1920s, as sketched by cartoonist Ern Shaw.

Tramcar to The Boulevard

I'm eighty now and I saw my first match in 1934, when I was fourteen. Joe Oliver, Dickie Fifield and Ernie Herbert were playing. We used to get a tramcar – it would cost me a halfpenny. Living close to the ground, The Boulevard was like a second home to me. Within two minutes I could be in the centre of the pitch. Being involved with the supporters' club brought us into contact with the players and we formed friendships. The supporters were more involved then. We used to clear the touchlines of snow and put straw down to protect the pitch. I remember one time stopping up all night and tending braziers to get the ground fit. We were closer to players then because they had jobs like us. I have Parkinson's disease now, but I used to go to the ground until two years ago and the directors were very good to me. I helped out in the office for about ten years.

Ernie Mason

Washing Days

My husband and I have been following Hull for fifty-odd years. I started going just after we'd been married, but Ernie had been going before then. I'm going back to the Eddie Caswell days when all our backyards used to be full of the team's washing that Mrs Caswell, the coach's wife, did in the dolly tub and a wringer. She lived next door to us in Graham Avenue, Airlie Street. All the neighbours used to lend a hand and hang them out. We lived right opposite the ground for fifty years. My husband used to go and sit in the stand and I'd be with my friends at the posh end.

Ivy Mason

Turkish Delight

My father's Turkish, but my mum's from Hull. It's strange for a Turkish man, but he's been supporting Hull for a long time and he started taking me when I was about two or three years old. When I was about nine I used to stand on a little chair to watch the match. I live in Leeds now but I never miss a match or an A-team game at The Boulevard.

Tim Pakyurek

It's a Religion

I'm a solicitor in Chester now, but I was born in Beverley and my father was born in Chester Grove, which is about 200 metres from The Boulevard. I've been going to watch Hull since I was about two or three with my father and grandfather. With living all his life so near to the ground, my grandfather used to be there every day talking to the players. His ashes are on the pitch just in front of the Threepenny Stand where he always stood. So I have mixed feelings about moving from The Boulevard to a new stadium. My dad has been following the club for over sixty years and I've been following them twenty-eight years. So, with my grandfather, we've got about 150 years of supporting Hull between the three of us. It's a religion in our house. I used to go to Sunday school, but since the age of five my dad was sending me down to play mini-rugby on a Sunday morning. I

Bert Gilbert becomes the first Australian captain to lift the Challenge Cup in 1914 .

Hull winger Billy Stone signs autographs for schoolboy fans at The Boulevard in 1920. Jim Humphries looks on.

speak to my dad on the phone now about two or three times a week and you can guarantee ninety-five per cent of the conversation is about Hull FC. He also sends me the sports pages from the *Hull Daily Mail* to keep me up to date.

Simon Shaw

A Link with the Past

I first went to see Hull in 1965 when I was ten years old and my dad took me. Then from 1968 I started going to all their home matches up until 1984 when I left Hull. I don't think I am ever likely to go back to live in Hull, but following the team is a strong link with the past. If I didn't go, I'd

feel part of my roots had gone. When they had a good team in the 1980s you think it is going to go on for ever and you have great expectations. They were great times with crowds of over 12,000. I remember thinking Hull have got to this from having crowds of about 1,000.

Keith Jenkinson

Sick Note to see Hull

My dad started to take me to watch Hull in 1972 when I was about eight. I remember my first game, it was against Blackpool Borough. We used to go in Threepenny Stand when it was quite easy to get in because there were only about a couple of thousand in the ground. My dad was there a few years earlier when there were only a few hundred for a match against Huyton. Years later, I reckon about 10,000 claimed they were there that day. At first I'd go with my dad all over. Then when I could go myself, I went with a few friends. Now I'm back going with my dad. I've often had to get a sick note from work to see Hull play. I've changed jobs since, so I can admit to it. I do shifts now and if they play midweek on my shift day, I've got to book a holiday to see them.

Stephen Buckley

Hooked on Excitement

I started going to see Hull about eleven years ago because my husband was a fan. I'd never been to a rugby match before, but when I met him I started going with him. I must admit that the first time I went, I thought what am I doing here, I'm really bored. But after the first season I was hooked. It was the atmosphere and everything about the game. It was so exciting. There was some swearing and that, but I've never felt intimidated at a game. It never bothered me at all. It was part of the rugby. I took it all in the fun it was meant to be. It's really my social life now. I live for the weekends. When my son was five we started taking him. We don't often miss an away match. I work at school on a dinner time with no weekends, so it's quite convenient to get to matches. We go to away matches on an organised bus. My husband works for East Yorkshire buses and most of the time he gets the away matches.

Kim Brindley

Classroom View

We'd get twopenny tickets at school to go see Hull. I went to Chiltern Street School, which was at the back of Threepenny Stand, and I can remember when Hull had a midweek match seeing the ball from the classroom window when it was kicked in the air. We could hear the crowd cheering and we'd think, oh Hull's scored. They must have been cup-tie replays that had to be played on midweek afternoons because there were no floodlights then. We went to see the first team one week and the A-team the next. After watching the A-team we'd go to the top of Bunker's Hill and wait for the loudspeaker to announce Hull's score away. Then we'd go home and about an hour later go to the corner of West Dock Avenue for a *Sports Mail* and read all about the match we'd just seen.

Harry Fletcher

Losing Start

I remember the first match I saw. It was a cup-tie against Barrow. I think it was in 1966. My father, who had been a Hull fan for a long time, took me and I've been going ever since. I don't remember much about the game except Hull lost. But it must have gripped me because I kept going back. I was about nine or ten and also playing for Ainthorpe, the school that Lee Crooks went to, so rugby was already becoming part of my life. I was there when Hull played Huyton and I think the crowd was about 800 on a Wednesday night. It was really depressing. I mean, at that time you had local amateur clubs like BOCM, Ambassador, Embassy and Hull Brewery getting crowds of that and

A rare action photograph of the great Billy Batten, passing to winger Jack Harrison.

and we've got to know each other. It's real friendly. I get really involved in the game now. I call the referee and all that. My other friends, who don't go to rugby, think I'm an oddball. 'What do you go to rugby for?' they say. They can't understand it. It's hard to say why I like it. I suppose it's the atmosphere. It's really good-humoured, and the game itself is great.

Carol Anderson

Tagging Along

I first started going to see Hull in the Eighties with my dad. He was Hull-mad. He'd been watching them since the Sixties and ran the coach trips now and again. One of his friends was Tony Duke, who used to hook for Hull. My brother used to go with them and a few others, so I just tagged along. I was ten at the time and I just got used to it gradually. Then I started playing for Andrew Marvell School and East Mount. I just liked the game totally. I went for quite a while at first, but then I stopped going about 1986. I don't know why. It might have been money, but I'd listen to matches on the radio. I started going again about five years ago and now I'm more keen than ever.

Mally Foston

Long Distance Fan

I started going about ten years ago when I was eighteen or nineteen. It was basically just wanting something to do on a Sunday. My dad used to go and still does religiously. I got hooked straightaway. It was just the

more on a Saturday afternoon. To go from that to seeing them play before 100,000 at Wembley was quite something.

Ian Anderson

Boulevard Courting Days

I used to go and watch Hull occasionally about twenty-two years ago because I was courting and he, my husband now, was really keen. He'd been going for years and gradually I started getting into it. I've started going every week since Hull went into Super League. It was a better game of rugby than what I'd seen before. It was nothing to do with summer rugby. It's practically winter weather all the time anyway. Now we're both season passholders and go to all the away matches on the Hull FC Supporters' coach. It seems to be the same group of fans atmosphere in Threepenny Stand, I think. Once you'd been you had to go again. I lived in Hull for twenty-five years and moved down to Nottingham to be with my girlfriend, now wife, who was at the university. But I still watch Hull FC as often as I can. When we go back to Hull, I always try to arrange it so that Hull are at home. And if there is any news about the team my dad will ring me about it.

Paul Ashton-Worsnop

Speedway Fan Converted

I started going to watch Hull in 1981. I used to watch speedway there and then a friend of mine said he was going to watch New Zealand play Hull at Boothferry Park. I went with him and I liked it immediately. It was the excitement, and the crowd made it as well. That was it for me. I was hooked and I've been going ever since. I never let the defeats get me down. As long as they do their best, there's always the next match.

Dave Worsnop

Family Tradition

My earliest recollection of going to see Hull was with my dad and my sister at Rovers. I don't remember it clearly, but I think we got there at half-time for some reason. It was at the new Craven Park and the ground was fairly empty compared with what derby games were normally like. I suppose I went because my dad, mum and sister had been Hull fans for a long time and so had my granddad. He was on the Board at one time

and the club treasurer. His name was Atkinson. So it was almost inevitable that I would follow. I was basically thrown into the whole rugby scene as a child of about seven and I'm been going ever since. I joined the Boulevard Kids, a group that had meetings with the players, and we got to know them. That was when Russ Walker, Greg Mackey, Lee Jackson, Richard Gay and Dean Busby were playing. It was a good time to be watching them. I sort of graduated from the Boulevard Kids area, standing at the scoreboard end and then to the Threepenny Stand, where I go now.

Craig Jessop

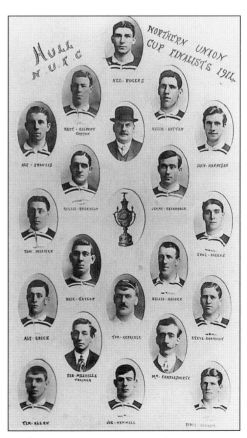

Hull's 1914 Cup-winning squad.

Jack Harrison posing in the Threepenny Stand. Two years after scoring a club record 52 tries in 1914/15, he was killed in action during the First World War and posthumously awarded the Victoria Cross.

A Fan at Four

I was about four when I first started watching Hull. That's twenty-four years ago. I went to The Boulevard with my parents and they took me to matches home and away. They'd been going for most of their life. It's a Hull FC family. I don't remember much about those early matches, but they obviously had a big effect on me because I've been going ever since.

Rob Dale

Gripped

I first started going about ten years ago when I was about seventeen, mainly because of my stepfather, who'd been going all of his life. I'd always followed Hull in the 'paper and went to watch them parade the Cup, but never went to matches because I was involved in cycle racing at weekends. Then I went with my stepfather and it gripped me straight away. I moved to Cleckheaton two years ago with work, but I still go to see Hull as often as possible, home and away.

Mike Beckett

Hull Fair Sideshow

My first ever match was when I went in at half-time with my auntie. I was about five. We were just walking by The Boulevard. We'd been to Hull Fair and lived only two streets from the ground. So we asked 'Can we go in and watch?' I don't remember anything else except that I had some candy floss and it went all over my auntie's shoe. But deep down the match probably had an effect on me and I really got into it in about 1979 when I started playing rugby at school.

David Boast

View from the Dugout

I started watching Hull about thirty-three years ago when I was four. My dad used to take me into Threepenny Stand and lay me on top of the coach's hut. Sometimes I'd sit on the bench with the players. When I started going with friends to The Boulevard, we'd walk from Bricknell Avenue to the match and walk home. It would be about three miles. There would be my friend, my sister and sometimes my cousins who would come to the house and we'd all go together to stand at the back of Threepenny Stand. It was a bit of a ritual and really got you going for the game. My daughter, who is twelve, and little son, who is eight, now go with me and for the last two years we've been to virtually every match home and away. My mother and father also go with us. It's a family thing.

Andy Scarah

Growing Passion

I've followed Hull for most of my life, but I've only started going regularly for the past five or six years and getting a season ticket. I started when I was about thirteen. I'd always been interested in rugby, playing for my school, St Mary's. Then my cousin, who watched them regularly, took me and it grew from there. But I'd been brought up on it and it was thrown on to me, like being told 'You will support Hull FC and hate KR'. I was born the year before FC and KR played at Wembley and I was always told about it. My parents, grandparents and especially my cousin were always talking about those days. My cousin was ten years older and as soon as I was born, apparently he kept telling me to like FC.

Matt Smith

Newcastle Soccer Fan Won Over

I'm a new convert. I started watching Hull only three weeks ago. I was brought up in

Hull captain Joe Oliver with the Yorkshire League and RL Championship trophies won in 1935/36.

the North East and we never had much to do with rugby league. I used to think rugby union was played by educated psychopaths and rugby league by working-class psychopaths. I remember when Hull met Rovers at Wembley and I was watching the news about some place called Hull and there was a big sign saying 'Last one out switch the light off.' But it meant very little to us. Then I met my wife and she used to take our young son, David, to watch Hull. But I still had no interest in it. I'd been in Hull about fifteen years and never been to a match. Then my wife had to attend a wedding in Scotland, so I had to take David. He has a season pass and if I didn't take him nobody would. It was the first time I had been to a rugby league match. It was against Wigan and the atmosphere reminded me of when I used to go to watch Newcastle at St James Park when I was a young 'un. I didn't understand what the players were doing, but I really enjoyed it. Then I went to the next match against Wakefield and away to watch them at Leeds. My wife said I must bring them luck because they'd never played so well since I started watching them. I soon got into it and now I wear the black and white shirt and feel part of a big family. I've also learnt *Old Faithful*, well at least the 'Giddy-up old fellah' bit.

Paul Young

Rovers Supporter Changes Colour

Originally I was from East Hull, so I was a Rovers supporter. There was always a rivalry between East and West, but even when I supported Rovers I didn't hate Hull. I've started going to watch Hull now because of my son David – he's ten, and really interested in it. Then I just got hooked as well, and I go because I like it now. It was the atmosphere of the crowd and the friendliness. I like supporting the team and wishing them well.

Christine Young

Keeping the Peace

I started going to watch Hull when my kids stopped going with my husband. I went to keep him company and keep him out of trouble because he used to argue with people. I had no particular interest at first and wondered why I was going. I still don't know a great deal about rugby, but now I

enjoy it. It's the excitement and atmosphere. We went in Threepenny Stand and still do in the old bit that's left. It was always packed then and if you turned sideways you couldn't turn back, it was that full.

Doreen Scarah

It Started in a Pub

I've been watching Hull since I was sixteen and I'm sixty-two now. It started when we were all sat in a pub. All my mates used to go to Hull one Saturday, and Hull City the next. I never went with them until one Saturday I said 'Oh, go on, I'll go with you'. It happened to be Hull and I've been going ever since. It got me straight away. I can't remember the match, but I remember the players – Whiteley, the Drakes, Scott, Finn, Broadhurst and Bateson. Not a bad team.

Barry Scarah

Every Match an Away Game

I was living in Grimsby when I started watching Hull as soon as I came out of the army in 1988. I've been watching them ever since, still travelling from Grimsby. Every match is like an away match for me. When they are at home I drive over to the ground and when they play away I drive over to pick the coach up. When I came out of the army it was just one of those things I wanted to do because I didn't have time when I was in to go and watch them. My parents are from Hull and my dad used to watch them, but he was in the RAF and drifted away from the game. He didn't talk a lot about Hull FC

Hull with the Yorkshire League trophy in 1936. They also won the RL Championship that year. From left to right, back row: Caswell (trainer), Overton, Booth, Stead, Dawson, Thacker, L. Barlow, Carmichael. Middle row: G. Barlow, Wilson, Corner, Oliver, Fifield, Miller. Front row: Herbert, Courtney. Inset: Ellerington, Gouldstone.

apart from when the fishermen used to come with crates of beer and pass it round. I was born abroad and only lived in Hull for about six or eight months. The first match I went to after I came out of the army was Hull against Rovers in a pre-season friendly and they were scrapping within about three minutes. I thought this looks fun. Chico Jackson hit somebody. It was right what they said about it being all blood and guts. And I loved it.

Graham Foot

Bug Bit at Wembley

I went to a few games in the late Seventies and I watched games on *Grandstand* on Boxing Day, when it always seemed to be Leeds playing with Eddie Waring doing the commentaries. But I started watching Hull regularly after they played Rovers at Wembley in 1980. That's what gripped me. I went to the final with a friend of mine who was a Rovers supporter. We just enjoyed the game and went round the town afterwards.

John Atkinson

Academy Link

I've only been watching Hull since my son joined their Academy side this season. We come from Doncaster and travel over to see him. I'd been a Doncaster fan, but since my son started playing for the Hull Academy

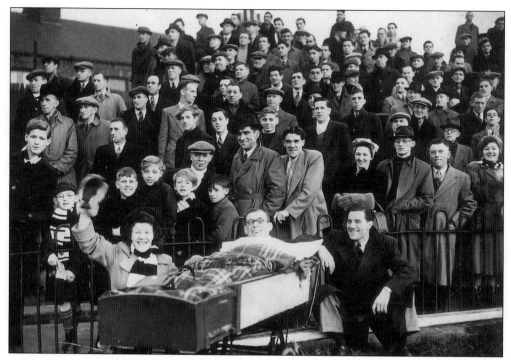

This invalid was a regular resident at Ryan's Corner in the early 1950s. Raymond Fletcher, compiler of this book, is the young fan with a black and white scarf near the centre of the carriage.

I've become a Hull supporter. To see him play in the first team would be a dream. But I think I would still follow Hull even if he wasn't playing for the Academy. They are a good team to watch.

Dawn Kirsopp

Going Against the Grain

I didn't start watching Hull until I moved to Leeds where my father worked about twelve years ago when I was sixteen. My first recollections of Hull FC are from when I was at primary school in Beverley. Both Hull and Hull K.R. were very strong, but the majority of the kids at school seemed to follow Rovers. So I took it upon myself to go against the grain and follow Hull. I got myself a Hull shirt and body warmer. That was my total involvement with Hull and I never actually saw any matches until I moved to Leeds. My first match was a John Player semi-final against Wigan at Headingley. I only went then because a friend at school was a Wigan supporter. I don't remember much about the game except it was a cold, dark, dingy day and I think Hull narrowly lost. I think I started watching Hull regularly because having left to live in Leeds, I wanted to keep in touch with my roots and the area. My grandparents still lived in Hull and they'd get cuttings from the *Hull Daily Mail* and send them to me.

Richard Wilson

Saturdays with Dad

I first started going to see Hull with my dad about twenty years ago when I was five. My parents had split up and I remember going down to my dad's house every Saturday and, with him being a big Hull fan, I would go with him to The Boulevard. I don't remember much about the matches, just bits like running onto the pitch after the match to congratulate them. It was winter rugby then and I remember being there with my big jacket on. My dad would stand on the terraces and I would go to the front, just to the right of Threepenny Stand, because I was quite small. I don't remember many of the players but I had Dane O'Hara's name on my shirt and I painted a big five on the back of my jumper. So I must have liked him as a little kid.

Mark Donoghue

Fifty Years a Fan

I've been to most home games for more than fifty years and many away. The only time I missed out a bit was between 1968 and 1972 when I was in Essex, but I'd still come back for the Yorkshire Cup final at Headingley and all the holiday games. I never stopped going. I have said 'What a shower' after a bad match, but always gone back the next week. The 1999 Super League season was a case in point. We just seemed to be going round in circles, but we still went. It's a religion. You try to go to every game. It's as simple as that.

Eric Gibbons

Winning Start

My first ever game was in 1979. It was a

Hull 1947/48. From left to right, standing: Booth, Tindall, Evans, Bedford, Ryan, Kavanagh. Sitting: Miller, Watt, Madden, Lawrence, Bowers, Sullivan, Jackson.

Floodlit Trophy match against Huddersfield. For some reason it had been re-arranged and played on a Sunday afternoon. We won 34-7, I think. I'd never seen a live game before, but Digger Dawson, who I played football with and drank in St John's pub in Queens Road, was a big FC fan and he took me. I had worked in Hull for two years before I got the bug. Hull won the Floodlit Trophy that year, beating Rovers in the final. I remember going to the final in December because it clashed with the office Christmas party and by going to the game first I missed the food.

Rob Lonsdale

Tommy Glynn, a Hull winger in the 1940s. Note the size of the ball.

Swept Off Her Feet

My mother was not really a fan, but her brothers were and she said they once all went together to The Boulevard and she was swept along by the crowd with her feet off the floor. She never stopped talking about that. I started going regularly from round about the Sixties with a few breaks as the kids came along. I'm a season ticket holder now and the two of us, my husband and me, go all over the place to watch them and the A-team.

Shirley Gibbons

Graduating as a Fan

The old Threepenny Stands will always have a special place for me. It was where I graduated as a supporter. I first went with my dad and he would leave me at the railings while he went up in the stands. The railings seemed to be just the right height because I can remember holding two spikes with my chin resting on a curved piece between them. Another thing that comes to mind was seeing little bits of fire in the grass near the touchline. I wondered what they were and then realised they were tab ends that people had flicked out over the railings. Then I can remember one day my dad saying I could go and stand with him. It was like a big part of my growing up. The three things that struck me about it were the smells of wood, the damp and cigarette smoke. It was like a pub atmosphere and I loved it. I remember that each tier of steps was quite high, so that I could see quite easily. I thought it was a really big stand, but years later I was surprised to find it quite small. I also remember the loudspeaker announcing best wishes to Hull FC from supporters at sea on trawlers.

Trevor Gibbons

Playground Rubble

I started going to watch Hull in 1949 when I was five because my dad and Uncle Bill went. I couldn't wait to go with them and went every week. My first recollection is of larking about among the rubble as they were building the new stand. As I got older we moved from the best stand to Threepenny Stand and stood there for many, many years. My biggest memory is of a Leeds forward, who came running off. I think he might have been sent off. Anyway, as kids, we shouted 'You can't play.' Then, as he went past us, he smacked me and broke my nose. He ran away into a Nissen hut at the back of the best stand, which was the changing rooms then. My dad and some of his mates went in and grabbed hold of him; they give him one. They worked on the docks and thought nothing of it. I'll never forget it and I can still bend my nose because I haven't got a bone in it. I think the player was transferred by Leeds not long after. It didn't stop me going and later on I became a vice-president.

Mike Adamson

Every One a Winner

My dad first took me to The Boulevard when I was about eight or nine years old, as my granddad had taken him when he was a lad. My earliest memories are of the 1978/79 season when Hull won all their Second Division

matches. I remember being at the last game against Hunslet. It was a low-scoring game, but we won to get the record. The ground was packed. We used to stand in Threepennies near the 25-yard line at Bunker's Hill end. I started watching near the railings and as I grew bigger I began standing further back on the steps, holding on to the stanchions until I got a bit older. I remember there used to be a ball boy who would have loads of packets of Polo mints and he'd throw them to old fellows in the crowd before the game.

Ian Roberts

Like Father, Like Son

I started going to The Boulevard with my grandfather in 1978 when I was about fourteen. The first game he took me to was against Rovers. I think that's why we all went, because it had been well-publicised. I don't remember much about it except that Hull won. So that was a good start and I've been going ever since. I started taking my lad when he was about seven. He'd watch half the game, but in the second half he'd lose interest and wander off. But he's ten now and really into it, telling me about the game. It's like when I went with my grandfather.

Mike Poole

First Match a Rib Crusher

I first went to see Hull in about 1928 when I was four or five years old. My father used to take me on his shoulders. I remember when he took me to Craven Park for a derby game. There must have been 20,000 and he got his ribs crushed coming out and finished up in

A training run in 1961. From left to right: Terry Hollindrake, George Matthews, Jack Kershaw, Mick Scott, Gordon Harrison and Tommy Finn.

the infirmary. The Coupland family were all mad rugby-ites and must have watched through all of the last century. There was one occasion when I was about seven when my father and uncle went to see Hull without me. They wouldn't let me go for some reason. But after they'd gone I ran all the way down St George's Road, down Massey Street and cut through the passage alongside the cemetery. By the time they'd got to the Threepenny Stand entrance, I was sat there waiting for them. When it was icy, me and a pal would go down early to run up and down the pitch to soften the ground up before the referee came. There would be a handful of us from West Dock Avenue School. I don't know what good we did with size four shoes.

Aubrey Coupland

Lasting Impression

The first time I went to The Boulevard was with my Uncle Ted and I saw Lewis Jones playing for Leeds. I don't remember what the score was, but this bald-headed full-back kicked goals from all over. You could have put him at the back of Threepenny Stand and he'd have scored from there. Because we lost my uncle clipped my ear hole and said that's the last time you go to The Boulevard with me. Another time I was running home from a match, which Hull had just won against the odds, when this copper stopped me in a Gordon Street and asked me who had won. When I said Hull, he hit me that hard with his cape I did a double somersault. He must have thought I was lying. The dugout them days was on the Threepenny Stand side opposite where the players came out and I'd sit on top of it watching the match. There'd be two or three other kids sitting with me.

Bob Cone

Old Faithful Spine Tingler

I bet everybody says this, but my dad first took me to see Hull probably when I was about ten or eleven. It was maybe a couple of years later that it really got to me when Hull played a semi-final against St Helens at Odsal. We weren't winning but the Hull fans started singing *Old Faithful*. It was awesome and the first recollection I had of the hair standing up on the back of my head and a tingle going down my spine just listening to it. That was what started it for me and I still get the same feeling now every time we sing it. My dad was born in Pontefract and was a Castleford fan. But he came to work on the docks in Hull. Rugby league was in his blood but not in Hull. But he started to watch them and eventually I went with him.

Steve Roberts

Peter Sterling, the great Australian Test scrum-half, makes a break against Castleford in the 1985 RL Challenge Cup semi-final.

CHAPTER 2

Boulevard Heroes

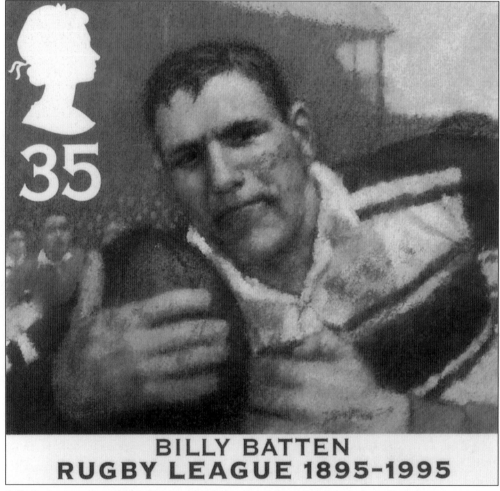

BILLY BATTEN
RUGBY LEAGUE 1895-1995

Billy Batten was one of five players to be depicted on postage stamps to mark the game's centenary in 1995.

Hero Delivered School Milk

Joe Oliver was one of our heroes when we were kids in the 1930s because he delivered our school milk. One of the Hull benefactors at that time were a family called Rymer and they had Riley's Dairy, who used to deliver milk to the schools. Of course, when Joe Oliver brought a crate of milk he was surrounded by all the kids. We used to play with a paper ball in the pouring rain in the school yard and seeing Oliver was a big thrill. We'd get our penny tickets from school to go see him play. He was a great player but I thought he was the greediest of centres and never gave his winger a chance. They'd freeze to death. I think Dickie Fifield, an Australian, also worked for Riley's Dairy because that was part of their contract when they signed, that they got a job with them. Freddie Miller was another hero. I remember him when he was only sixteen. He became a really big kicker of the ball. He would often attempt a drop goal from the halfway line and when he got a free kick near his own line the ball would finish up in the other team's quarter. But there were a lot of big kickers then, usually the full-back, and there would be kicking duels from corner to corner. They could put side on the ball. It was wonderful to watch and Miller was one of the best. A school pal of mine at West Dock Avenue School was Willie Allen, who was captain of our team. He played for a Hull when he was sixteen, a wonderful prodigy as a centre, but he went into the Forces and never came back. I also went to school with the Bedfords, Ted and Arthur. Both played rugby and Arthur, who was about my age, turned out to be quite a good forward for Hull. I also remember their mother, a big woman who was a Hull

Frank Boylen, a member of Great Britain's first touring squad to Australia and New Zealand in 1910, shows off his array of representative caps.

supporter. One day she came to school on open day at West Dock Avenue and asked one of the teachers, 'Bogey' Seltzer, who was a really hard man, if they were behaving. And when he said they were, she said: 'Well, if they don't, belt the buggers.' I remember Ginger Stead pre-war. He was a rough dock lad but clean-living like they all seemed to be then. I knew somebody who met him in Alexandria, in Egypt, during the war and said he was in charge of the docks there as Major Stead. He was a hard man who worked his way to the top. Later I got to know Bruce Ryan because he had his hair cut at the same place I went, Louis Rubens. Ryan was the manager of Austin

BATTEN'S THREE TRIES.

SUCCESSFUL DEBUT WITH HULL IN MATCH AGAINST KEIGHLEY.

Scorers.—Hull: Batten (3), Gilbert (2), Herridge (2), Harrison (2), and G. Rogers, tries; E. Rogers (3), Darmody (2), goals.
Keighley, Pickles, try.

Thanks in a very large measure to the inclusion of W. Batten, the ex-Hunslet captain, in their ranks for the first time, Hull ran up their largest account of the season at the Boulevard. Keighley, who were the victims, played pluckily, however, and finished with only eleven men. Cole was dismissed, and Wilson had to retire owing to severe injury. The odds were thus heavily against Keighley, who were beaten by the pace and general cleverness of the home backs, and Batten in particular. The latter player not only helped himself to a trio of tries, but made the running for at least three others.

Matters did not work altogether smoothly for Hull at the start, this being due to some very determined tackling by the visiting backs. Taylor, Watson, and Farrer were particularly smart in this respect, and with just a little more pace they might have accomplished something even more effective. It could not be claimed that the winners excelled in the scrimmaging department, the forwards being well matched in this respect. Harrison was the most successful winger, Batten constantly getting his immediate companion into action.

Altogether Batten's debut was most successful, and his work was often deservedly applauded by a crowd of 8,000 people. Hull have long needed a forceful and scoring centre three-quarter, and the International promises to participate in a very successful wind up to the season's engagements at the Boulevard.

Though his permit to play against Keighley was only a provisional one, pending the inquiry into his transfer, the Hull club are very confident about enjoying the permanent services of the ex-Parksider.
NAUTICUS.

A report of Billy Batten's debut for Hull in 1913 after his sensational signing from Hunslet for a then staggering £600 record transfer fee.

Reeds, an immaculate, smart fellow with black curly hair, film star looks and a fine physique – a real ladies' man who made them all swoon. But he was idolised by all Hull fans. Apart from all that he was a great winger. He could run, sidestep and was a wonderful ball handler. He didn't really need a centre and would go inside looking for the ball.

Aubrey Coupland

Australians were Brilliant

It was great when Hull had a few Australians in the early post-war years, like George Watt, Bruce Ryan and Duncan Jackson. They were brilliant. We played against Bradford once when Watt was sent off and Jackson broke a collarbone. Then one of the Bedford brothers got sent off and we still beat them with ten men. We had just three players packing down in the scrum. No substitutes then, of course. I was about eleven and I saw Jackson after the match because I was collecting autographs and he came out with his arm in a sling. Ryan was the best of them all. He was so fast and the star of the game after the war. Ivor Watts was a good little winger. He'd run at full speed and put in a crossfield kick all at once. He never paused to look, just did it all in one go. Arthur Keegan was a great full-back. I'll never forget Keegan standing on the twenty-five yard line on the Threepenny Stand side near our favourite spot at the Airlie Street end. The great Billy Boston came running down the wing and Keegan thudded him straight into touch. He was the only man I ever saw take Boston in full pelt. I don't think it did Keegan much good, though, because he wasn't quite well for the rest of the match.

Eric Gibbons

Give it to Ryan

I'll never forget Bruce Ryan. He was an Australian sprinter and I think he broke the 100 yards record. He was a powerful winger with a hand off like a mule.

Sullivan, his centre, scored a bag of tries just by using Bruce as a foil. He used to show the ball, look at Bruce and race up the field. Unfortunately, I don't think Bruce fitted in at Hull FC. I think the media had a lot to do with that. I well remember Bruce going to one or two reporters and asking if they would just tone it down a bit because it was 'Ryan this and Ryan that' in the papers. They were only writing about him and nobody else. But the coach Eddie Caswell, or trainer as it was then, used to end his team talk by saying 'I've only one more thing to say lads – get the ball to Ryan'.

Ernie Mason

Bomber Ahead of His Time

Tommy Harris may not have been the best hooker for getting the ball from the scrums, but he was ahead of his times in the loose. He just used to bomb through. That's why they called him Bomber Harris. I can seem him breaking down the middle and then sending a long pass right out to the wing. He didn't seem to look. He just threw it and it would go straight to the winger. My biggest memory of Jim Drake is of him charging into players and banging them in the face with the ball. He maybe only did it once but that's what I remember. Hull had a great pack of forwards then and that's when you could keep the ball for ages. So at times Hull would let the other side have the ball and tackle them so hard. Then after a bit you'd hear the Hull forwards shout 'Come on they don't want it. It's our turn now'. They'd had enough.

Harry Eve

A Great Winger

I always thought Bruce Ryan was a great winger. He wasn't a sidestepper. But he had this swerve and used to go right over on his side. A lot of his tries were from about 25 yards out. He was a well-built kid and so strong. It was his timing. He could judge when to move towards and away from a tackler. And if he didn't get a pass, he'd go looking for the ball. The crowd would expect something every time Ryan got the ball. We used to watch him in training or see him in the street. We'd point him out and say 'Look, Bruce Ryan'. Then we'd follow him down Boulevard. There was something about him that set him aside

Australian winger Frank Hurley, pictured soon after signing for Hull in 1937.

Ernie Herbert, Hull's stand-off in their 1935/36 Championship-winning season.

support and seemed to know just where it was. He seemed to have so much time. I'd just come out of the army then and we'd go down to Picky Park to watch Hull train. Whiteley was a Test player then and you knew he was special. He just looked good. It was his whole demeanour. He stood out. Little things like he used to play with his collar pulled up and wear really short shorts. He always looked a lot taller than the rest.

Harry Fletcher

Don't Forget Sykes

Johnny Whiteley was brilliant. He was one of those players who would have been brilliant in any era. But the forgotten man out of all them was Cyril Sykes. He was the other second row with Bill Drake. He was part of the team and as good as the others. But when you talk about that team now nobody mentions him. They always mention the other forwards. Maybe it's because he was the only one of the pack who wasn't an international. But he should have been. He was good enough. I remember when Clive Sullivan made his debut on one wing and Wilf Rosenberg made his debut on the other wing. The backs scored all the tries and it was the first time for years that a forward hadn't scored. Sullivan scored a hat-trick, but he was a trialist and played as A.N. Other. They wouldn't give his name. All they would say is that he had a famous name, but wouldn't say what it was. Well, Mick Sullivan played for St Helens then and it was only after the match that Hull gave out Clive Sullivan's name. I knew he was going to be good. You could see it straight away. I remember him scoring seven tries at Doncaster – a club record. I also

from the rest. A real handsome fellah. Johnny Whiteley is another player who stands out. One incident that I remember is him getting a breakaway and when the full-back came across to tackle him, Whiteley handed him off. It was the way he did it. The kid thought he had him and Whiteley sort of high-stepped and pushed him down. A great hand off. And he had this pass which he just whipped out. But that came later. When he was younger he was mainly a runner with a great style, sort of running on his toes. And when he broke out into the opening he was always looking round for liked Rosenberg, a South African. I liked the way he dived for the line, even when there was nobody near him. Now everybody does it, but he was the first.

Barry Scarah

Great Hand Off

Dick Gemmell was one of the best centres I saw play for Hull. It was the way he carried himself, the way he moved. I remember him coming down Threepenny Stand side and he could time his hand off so suddenly that the tackler was just smacked out of the way. Yet he never seemed to look at a player and would give no indication of which way he was going to move. He'd turn his head the opposite way to where he was going. Terry Hollindrake, what a sidestep. But too slow. He once beat the great Vollenhoven and the crowd cheered, but Vollenhoven still had time to turn round, race past him and tackle Hollindrake from the front. Wilf Rosenberg was a great little winger, very brave. He'd put his head back and go straight for the line. He was a South African, but I remember another South African who never made it. Pin McMillan got a lot of publicity, but he was a bit of a joke. He just didn't look the part. When he chased a loose ball he was like a chicken with his head nodding at it. He was quite tall and that made him look even worse. I don't think he ever played for the first team.

Harry Joseph

A Few Hard Cases

When Hull played Wigan at Wembley I remember little Ivor Watts saying: 'I'll stop Billy Boston if nobody else can'. Boston was a big winger and I can picture him now running down the wing with the ball under one arm and Ivor Watts under the other. At least that's how I imagined it. Paul Woods, what a hard case he was. He used to say 'What's a sidestep?' He didn't know, because he just ran at players. Lee Crooks was a tough player, but he always said he was glad to have Woods on his side because he was one player he wouldn't have liked to play against. He was an animal. But he was well liked by the fans because he wouldn't take a backward step. He could be

HULL WEAKNESS IS THE SCRUM

By KINGSTONIAN

HULL'S defeat at Dewsbury was no disgrace. It was largely due to the old fault of not getting the ball from the scrums, combined with opposition from a very dour defence.

Apart from this unfortunate position in set scrums the forwards played magnificently.

RYAN'S ARTISTRY

The Dewsbury crowd roared loud applause for Gilbertson when, with a half field-length run, he opened the home account, but their loudest cheer of the day was for Bruce Ryan.

During one of the Dewsbury periods of pressure the Australian took the ball almost on his own line and was away up the field. When Ledgard challenged Ryan beat him with a classic double-swerve and went over the line three yards ahead of the nearest Dewsbury defender.

A Hull Daily Mail *report of a length of the field try by Bruce Ryan in only his second match for Hull gives an early indication of the treats in store for Boulevard fans.*

a bit of a joker as well. I remember him taking a goal kick from near touch on the Threepenny Stand side and he only had about two yards to run up. So he took the ball further in field and the referee told him to put it back where it was. So Woods walked back and climbed over the barrier and pretended to start the run up from there. He was a bit of a character and was just having a go at the referee. In those days you never saw a rugby match that didn't have a punch up. They used to take it turns. I heard a story about one of the Drakes. It was his turn to smack somebody and as they were coming onto the field, Mick Scott said to him 'OK, don't forget the first chance you get smack such and such a player.' And either Bill or Jim Drake went after this player as they were coming out of the tunnel. They asked him what he was doing and he said 'You told me to smack him'. They said 'I know, but wait until the match starts.' And I remember Cyril Sykes, who used to play for Hull but went to Doncaster. He was playing for Doncaster when he tackled Terry Devonshire in front of Threepenny Stand and sat on him. He had him by the scruff of the neck, looked up at the crowd and asked 'Shall I smack him?' The crowd just laughed and shouted something worse back.

Bob Cone

Whiteleys Remembered

I remember Johnny Whiteley and his brother Peter. My friend's sister married Peter Whiteley, who had Bucky Club. The thing I remember about Johnny is that he was big and Peter was real skinny. Johnny

stood out from the crowd. Later there was Sammy Lloyd. He was good-looking, wasn't he? Everybody loved him. He took my brother's pub, the Lord Nelson, over when he died. My brother was a Rovers supporter and if he'd known Sammy Lloyd had taken it over he would have turned in his grave.

Doreen Scarah

The Flying Dentist

I used to love watching the 'Flying Dentist', Wilf Rosenberg. When I was a kid I had a picture in a rugby league magazine of Rosenberg scoring a try and he was diving for the line. He was horizontal and must have been four or five feet off the ground with a defender going underneath him. He was a hero of mine. There were other heroes like Arthur Keegan, Terry Kirchin, Joe Brown and Chris Davidson. I thought Kirchin was a marvellous ball handler. He was a tall, rangy second rower and a bit like Knocker Norton in what he could do with the ball, slipping it out of impossible situations. Norton was one of the best. Everybody said he was a great attacking player, which he was, but I liked his defensive play. He was hard as nails. He had everything.

Steve Roberts

Keegan Stood Alone

My first hero was Arthur Keegan. My early memory, right or wrong, is that Keegan seemed to stand between Hull and many defeats. I also remember Clive Sullivan and Mick Harrison as being very good players.

Keith Jenkinson

Like a Racehorse

My first hero was Clive Sullivan. He was the Great Britain captain but perhaps the real reason he was my hero is simply that he was a winger and therefore nearest to me where I stood on the Threepenny side. He used to have legs that he'd put oil on and it would make him look like a racehorse, all sinewy and shiny. I don't know how fast he was compared to players today but he seemed very fast. He was one of the best wingers I ever saw for coming back and covering a break on the other wing. He would turn and run diagonally across the field to clatter the opposing winger just short of the try line. He seemed to do that every game. An unlikely hero was Don Robson. I bet not many people would bring him to mind. But he always impressed me. The reason why he stuck out was a childhood, boyish sort of thing. I broke my elbow on my paper round and went to Hull Royal Infirmary. I was sat there waiting for an X-ray or something and the bloke next to me had his ankle in plaster. It was Don Robson. I doubt whether he would have been recognised by that many people, so we had a little chat. We shared broken bones and that seemed fantastic to me.

Trevor Gibbons

Forgotten Heroes

One of my first heroes is probably not remembered by many now. That was Jimmy Crampton. When he was signed from New Hunslet I thought he was the most free-scoring, free-running second rower I'd seen. I don't know why he made such an impression on me but he did. He played in the 1976 team

Johnny Whiteley, one of Hull's greatest and most popular players.

that got to the John Player final and is still my favourite Hull team of all time. They all looked a bit undernourished. I look at that team picture now and think they look a right bunch of misfits. But they played fantastic rugby. Another of that team to make a big impression on me was George Robinson. I suppose he is another to have been forgotten by most people, but not me. He must have weighed only three stones wet through with an unruly mop top of hair. He looked quite the most unlikely player, but he could tackle. He would stand there and some big forward would come running at him. Then somebody would always shout 'Use your weight George'.

Tony Gibson

Homage to Sullivan

My early heroes were Steve Norton and Dane O'Hara, I've got a photograph of me with O'Hara. And for some reason I remember Kevin James making his debut and scoring after combining with Garry Schofield. But the one who stood out was Clive Sullivan. I remember my dad taking me to Bradford and Bingley Building Society on Holderness Road, where he used to work, to get his autograph. My dad died and now when I go to the crematorium in Chanterlands Avenue to remember him I always stop by and have a look at Clive Sullivan's plaque. And when I take the kids to look at my dad's name in the book of remembrance I always point out Sullivan's plaque and say 'There's a great player for you'. I've got a few videos with him on, playing for Rovers and Hull.

Mally Foston

Mick Scott, Hull's captain when they won the championship in 1955/56.

The Blond Bombshell

Keith Boxall stood out because he had a shock of blond hair. But he was also a very good forward. He not only scored tries, but kicked goals and seemed to be everywhere at that time. One of my favourite all time away games was when we played Salford in a semi-final. I can remember standing with hundreds of Hull fans, singing and willing Hull to do something. That would be the first time they had done anything since winning the Yorkshire Cup about seven years earlier. Boxall scored a couple of tries I think, certainly kicked some goals and just seemed to be everywhere that day. He was a slightly tubby, barrel-like forward but he could run. Quite a few years later, I was on a North Sea Ferry going over to Holland and Boxall was on the same boat. I was with somebody who knew Keith and he introduced me to him. It was weird because I was grown up by then and it was twelve years since he'd been running around as my hero. But I couldn't manage anything other than 'Hello'. I wanted to tell him he was my hero and I remembered this, that and the other but I couldn't. Then he just said 'Hello' and walked off with his pint.

Terry Garner

Coach the Hero

When I was growing up we had the New Zealanders playing for us – Kemble, O'Hara, Ah Kuoi and Leuluai. Then we had Australian Peter Sterling when we had that great team in the Eighties. But my hero was not a player but a coach – Brian Smith, the fellow who turned the club round in the late Eighties, early Nineties. On the back of that he turned players from Hull like Lee Jackson, Andy Dannatt and Paul Eastwood from ordinary players into Great Britain internationals and at the same time put the club back on the map. So out of all the people that have pulled on the shirt or been associated with the club he would be my hero.

Tim Pakyurek

Photo to Treasure

My early heroes were players in the team that got to the 1976 John Player final. George Clark was my favourite player then and I remember being taken to Boyes department store to meet the players. There was a picture in the *Hull Daily Mail* of me with my black and white bobble hat on and National Health glasses with George Clark. That's my proudest picture. We've got the original from the *Hull Daily Mail* and I've got it signed as well. Then the memories start from when Arthur Bunting took over with players like Vince Farrar, Charlie Stone and my idol then, Steve 'Knocker' Norton. But I thought the greatest player of all time was Peter Sterling. I played scrum-half myself and I was fortunate enough to meet him a couple of times. During that 1982 Kangaroos' tour

A smoke and autograph session for Hull hooker Tommy Harris after playing for Great Britain against New Zealand at Bradford in the 1960 World Cup.

I kept a full scrapbook and I managed to get it signed.

Simon Shaw

Knocker the Tops

Favourite player? Give me my Knocker (Steve Norton). Joe Oliver was one of my first and Freddie Miller. I'm going back years. We used to go in Freddie Miller's pub. I used to think Paul Prendiville was lovely. He might not have been the greatest player, but he was a lovely lad, really friendly. They all used to come into the supporters' club in them days, you see. They weren't separate

35

like they are now. Bruce Ryan was another lovely chap and Duncan Jackson and George Watt – all Australians. I still see George Watt pushing his bike with the groceries in Gipsyville. Ryan was nicely spoken and a real good-looking guy. And I loved Johnny Whiteley. Nice lad was John and still is.

Ivy Mason

Brilliant Boxall

They were struggling when I first watched them. Then Hull started to sign the top brand names: Steve Norton, Sammy Lloyd,

The Drake twins, members of Hull's mighty pack of the 1950s: Jim (left) and Bill.

Vince Farrar, Charlie Stone and all them. That was the start of the big days. But my first hero was Keith Boxall. I thought he was a brilliant forward. He really grafted and kicked goals as well. I remember Clive Sullivan as a great player who scored some terrific tries. And I remember us getting Steve Evans for a record £72,000. We couldn't believe it. It was a lot of money then.

Stephen Buckley

Crane Could Have Been a World-Beater

I had no particular heroes, but I remember Arthur Keegan as a full-back nobody could get past. I also remember Howard Firth because he was a coach at our school. He was a bit of a sprinter, a will o' the wisp, and could move. But I never thought him a proper rugby player. Mick Crane was a player with certain skills that could win games. He maybe wasn't as dedicated as he should have been, but if he had been he would have been a world-beater. Dave Topliss and Peter Sterling would have to be among the best I've seen. Great half-backs. If the half-backs are controlling the game, they can win it for you. Sterling wasn't with us for very long, but he was special with players running off him. I work with Jim Drake, who used to play for Hull years ago. He's part-time in the fruit trade and a real gentleman. I'm told he wasn't like that on the field, but he is now. He doesn't talk much about the game unless he's asked.

Ian Anderson

Three of the Best

Three players who come to mind are Gary Kemble, Steve Norton and Steve Prescott. Prescott because he was the outstanding player when we had a bad season a year or two ago. He kept things ticking over. Norton was just a very skilful player. If he was around now he would still be up there among the best. He would have upped his game for Super League and his ball skills would have been as good as anybody's today.

Dave Worsnop

A Treasured Gift

My sister is a diabetic and when she was in hospital Lee Jackson brought his number nine shirt in and gave it to her. The number nine is torn at the back, but I think it's just amazing. It's the old style shirt and that's how I see Hull. Every now and then I take it out and put it on. It's got this magic.

Craig Jessop

Magical Norton

Steve Norton was a magical player. He had so many skills. He could waltz round players, side-step them and had such great balance. He was a very clever footballer. He was the key signing that started Hull on their way to success in the 1980s.

Peter Oglesby

Clive Sullivan MBE, scored a record 250 tries for Hull.

Dean Put His Body on the Line

Steve Norton was my first hero. Also Tony Dean, who was an underrated player. I really rated him because he always put his body on the line. He was a very brave, clever player and did so much work. James Leuluai was another of my favourites and Fred Ah Kuoi. Some of the tries Leuluai scored were tremendous, especially the one against Castleford in the Cup semi-final and the final against Wigan. They were brilliant and very similar tries.

Rob Dale

Hasler had Class

My favourite player must be Des Hasler, the Aussie. He was only here two years, but I remember his class and a try when he virtually ran through the whole opposing team. He was probably past his best when he came to Hull, so he must have been a really great player at his peak playing for Australia.

Mike Beckett

Hardest Tackler

One of the hardest tacklers I ever saw was Trevor Skerrett. I can still remember the best tackle I've ever seen to this day. It was by Skerrett on Castleford's Keith England in the semi-final. He nearly broke him in half. What a tackle. I've never seen one like it. It was the most clean and hardest tackle I've ever seen. When we're in the pub talking and it gets round to what was the best tackle we've seen, the Hull fans always come out with this one. There's one kid who has got it on video and he watches it every week still. Mick Crane was a good larker. He had a great set of hands. He lived only half a mile from us. We were on Bransholme Estate and he lived in Sutton. When he brought the Cup home, I had my photograph took with it.

David Boast

Macklin a Character

My main memory would be watching Alf Macklin running up and down the wing when I first started to watch Hull. He wasn't a great player but he was a character and

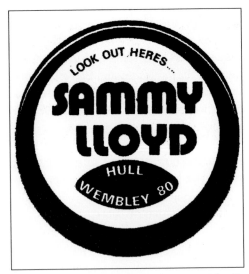

A badge that reflected Sammy Lloyd's popularity.

people tend to talk about him more than some of the better players. There was just something about him I liked. Perhaps it was just because he was a winger and the nearest player to me when I started watching Hull. He was a good, solid winger who was always there and he was a Hull lad. I've seen him play darts since around town and it's interesting to see him again.

Andy Scarah

Missed Debut

Trevor Skerrett was a good player and I remember his debut – because I didn't see it. It was at Leeds and some of us Hull fans from The Tiger pub in Cottingham hired a mini-bus. But it ran out of petrol before we had even left Cottingham. Eventually, we arrived ten minutes after the kick-off to discover Skerrett had already been sent off. A great individual performance I remember was by Mick Sutton against Leeds at The Boulevard. Mick came off the bench after twenty minutes to play the game of his life and deservedly win the Man of the Match award. He tackled like a demon, pushing Leeds back every time and making great yards whenever he had the ball.

Kevin Horsley

Chico Made Big Impression

Chico Jackson made an early impression on me because of his broken nose. He never gave a quarter and was one of those blokes who always gave 100 per cent if not more. I

Sammy Lloyd, a great favourite with Hull's young fans.

like that type of player. There may be better players, but he was one you could really rely on when it got tough.

Graham Foot

Norton the Best

Steve Norton would have to be the player who stands out the most. In the twenty years or so that I have watched Hull, he was without doubt the best player I've seen. It was his ball-handling skills. He just used to mesmerise people. They seemed completely bamboozled by him. He could go by them by just throwing a dummy. They just couldn't read him. Dave Topliss was a terrific player, and the best full-back Hull ever had was Gary Kemble without a doubt. He could field a ball anywhere. He very rarely dropped one.

John Atkinson

Kiwis had Best Legs

I liked the Kiwis who played for Hull in the Eighties. You couldn't beat the set of legs that Dane O'Hara, Gary Kemble and James Leuluai had.

Shirley Gibbons

Hard As Nails

I remember them signing Jimmy Crampton. That started the big signings. Then came Sammy Lloyd, Knocker Norton and the Kiwis. They were among my first heroes. But Knocker has to be the one. He's

James Leuluai steps out at The Boulevard for his debut in 1981.

I think he could have been if he had applied himself. He had the talent to be as good as he wanted to be. But he'd turn up at training smoking, liked a drink and that sort of thing. He was a real character. I had a vision of what he must look like away from matches, you know, a bit scruffy. But he came to one of the fans' meetings a few months ago to have his honorary membership of the Independent Supporters' Association picked up and he looked like an affluent tanned businessman dressed up in his suit.

Ian Roberts

Stone a Legend

The player I remember most from my earliest days of watching Hull, and who is still a big hero, is Charlie Stone. I met him at a dinner recently and I told him he was a legend. I was in awe of the guy, but he said 'Don't be daft lad'. He was one of those players who don't get full credit for what they do. He brought a lot of young players on with his total leadership. Players like Lee Crooks, who became a great forward. What I liked about Charlie Stone is that he led the pack and put everything into it. He was a miner then in the Featherstone area and used to go down the mines before a match and start an early shift so he could be back in time for the kick-off. Imagine that. Starting at five in a morning so that he could finish at one o'clock and get to Hull for the game. Now some of these soccer players can't play two games a week.

Mike Poole

probably the best player I've seen in a Hull shirt. There was just something about him. David Maiden was reminiscent of him early this season, getting the ball away in a tackle and being elusive. Knocker was as hard as nails as well. I can always remember singing 'Knocker's going to get you' if there was any trouble. He was the enforcer. He had sublime skills, but he could also knuckle it. He looked the part with bumps on his head and I was shocked when I heard him speak because he's got quite a high-pitched voice. I expected him to be real gruff. There's lots of stories about Mick Crane and his antics. I thought he was a class player but I might have missed him at his best. He wasn't as good as Knocker, but

Schofield Was Special

The young Garry Schofield scored some great tries. The times he used to get the ball in his own half and away he went. He had something special from the day he started. He had terrific pace and was a poacher. I was quite disappointed when he left. It broke the back of the club at the time. It really hurt the club when he left. But I still regard him as one of the game's greats as much as we hate him.

Andy Scarah

Didn't Look the Part

It's funny how some players stick out in your memory even though they probably weren't outstanding players. There was a guy called Les Baxter in the Fifties. He was a forward but didn't look like a rugby player. I think he used to squint a bit and it was said he was half blind. I don't know if he could play but he made some sort of impression on me as a school kid. There was another called Hand and I thought that was funny because he was a hooker when handing the ball out of the scrum was quite common.

Ron Freeman

Tony Dean takes on Hull K.R. in the 1981 Premiership Trophy Final at Headingley. Colleague Mick Crane looks on.

Garry Schofield watches Lee Crooks score a try against Hull K.R. in 1983.

A Pack of Stars

There's a whole pack of players that I remember. They were the forwards that made Hull such a feared team in the Fifties. They come easily to mind. Mick Scott was at prop. He captained them when they won the championship in 1956. He started in the first team as a teenager and always looked quite boyish although he was a big guy. The other prop was Bob Coverdale and later Jim Drake. What a contrast. Coverdale was called the Mayor of Dunswell after the village where he lived and looked much older than he was. He had a craggy face but wasn't a rough player. Not like Jim Drake, who was one of the hardest forwards I ever saw – alright, dirty at times. He started as full back in the A team, but put a lot of weight on because of

glandular fever or something. Then he was a tank, a real tough nut. His twin brother Bill played in the second row and was different altogether, a great footballer with a clever dummy and ball distribution. On his best days he could be as good as Johnny Whiteley, who was the prince of them all. Harry Markham was the other second row, a big hard-boned runner. Whiteley was an athlete of pure class. In the middle of that lot was Tommy Harris, a hooker well ahead of his time. He was one of the first hookers who could really get about in the loose and had a terrific sudden burst of speed. He would have been sensational in today's game. Cyril Sykes came later and was not quite in the same class as the others but a real worker.

Charles Arnold

Flattered to Deceive

Does anybody remember Patrick O'Leary? He played about fifty years ago. Despite the name I think he was a Welshman. He was quite an exciting and fearless full-back. When he was waiting to field a high ball he would lick his finger tips in anticipation. Then he'd catch the ball and set off in a daredevil style. He was a curly haired, really fit-looking guy. Yet I think he died quite young. One of the greatest prospects I ever saw was a young kid called Pat Skinner. He was a half-caste with black glossy hair and was absolutely brilliant. I first saw him when he played for Hull Juniors in curtain-raisers in the Fifties. People used to go early to Hull's matches just to see him play for the juniors. He was sheer class, a bit like the young Ellery Hanley. He had a sleek running style and would tease the opposition with dummies. He had the lot. Hull signed him on, but he never made the grade. Apparently his attitude wasn't right and he just faded away. What a waste of talent. I remember another teenager who made a great impression. George Matthews was an amateur international from Barrow and he made a very impressive debut for the A team. Quite a few thousand turned up for the game and everybody was talking about him afterwards. Hull had a great pack then but no class backs and we thought Matthews had been sent from Heaven. But he turned out to be just a very good club player. The best thing he did was score all three tries when Hull beat Featherstone in the 1959 semi-final to get Hull to Wembley for the first time.

Ron Ford

George Matthews scores the first of his three tries in Hull's RL Challenge Cup semi-final defeat of Featherstone in 1959.

CHAPTER 3
Memorable Tries and Matches

Hull's New Zealand trio lead the Haka to celebrate winning the championship in 1983. From left to right, front row: Gary Kemble, James Leuluai and Dane O'Hara.

Bruce Ryan, an outstanding Australian winger who was a big favourite with Hull fans in the 1940s.

The Best and Funniest

One of the best tries I remember was scored by a winger Hull signed from South Wales, Gouldstone I think, in the 1930s. He was the fastest winger that's ever been on The Boulevard. Hull were losing to Salford, a great team then, and all of a sudden Gouldstone got the ball on his own line and set off. When Salford players came across, he just chipped the ball over their heads, raced down the touchline, took the ball on the bounce and went over under the sticks. I think Hull won 5-4. I've never seen my father so excited. He took his hat off , threw it in the air and never saw it again. I remember a funny try scored against Hull when the ball was kicked past Tom Hart, our full-back. He went back for it and looked round to see who was chasing him. Then as he bent to pick the ball up he accidentally kicked it back another ten yards. He went back to try to pick it up again and kicked it out of his own hands again, like a comedy. It went over his own line and an opposing player raced up and touched it down.

Aubrey Coupland

Ryan's Try

The try I remember most was Bruce Ryan's against New Zealand in 1947. It's still a talking point. Even now when I talk to old pals about it, they say 'Oh, I remember that, I was there'. It started on the Threepenny Stand side at the Gordon Street end. I was

EXPECTANT HUSH AS HUTTON'S KICK SAILS FOR THE POSTS TO BRING THE CHAMPIONSHIP TO HULL AFTER A 20-YEAR WAIT

Colin Hutton kicks the late match-winning goal that won the 1956 Championship Final against Halifax at Maine Road, Manchester.

on Bunker's Hill. There was a scrum. Jackson got the ball out and Ryan came inside and started to run across to the other side of the field. Memories play tricks with you, but I can see him in my mind's eye, going away from me. It was so dramatic. It wasn't a fluke, or an interception, or just a breakaway. He had to make it all himself and he just swerved round them. There was nothing happening until Ryan got the ball.

I remember little incidents more than great matches. It's funny, but the matches I remember most is when they got beat. There was one at Bradford when they lost to St Helens in a semi-final. We were doing all right and it was Vollenhoven who beat us with a great try. I'll never forget that. Mick Scott tried to take his head off but nobody could stop him. Another incident that sticks out is when Hull played Halifax at Headingley in a Yorkshire Cup final and

Keith Bowman scored the equalising try late in the game. There was a photo sequence of the try in the paper. Maybe that's why I remember it. And I remember Halifax's Wilkinson coming off the field with blood streaming down his face. There had been a real bust-up at a scrum. They'd packed down and somebody came flying out of the scrum. Then they packed down again and somebody else came flying out.

Harry Fletcher

Slow Handclap for Creeping Barrage

I can remember the first time I heard the slow handclap at a rugby match. It was when Hull played Workington in a Cup-tie at The Boulevard in 1954. The pitch was a heavy bog and Workington had just drawn level at 5-5 with twenty minutes to go and decided to settle for a replay back up in Cumbria. Those were the days of unlimited play-the-balls and Workington stuck the ball up their jerseys. Hull tried everything to get it back. They even deliberately walked off side to be penalised, because a penalty kick to touch then was followed by a scrum and they had a good chance of winning possession. But that didn't work. Workington just kept barging forward without passing. It was called the creeping barrage. That's when I heard it. The slow handclap started going right round the ground from about 20,000 fans. It made no difference. Workington stuck at it to the end to earn a replay.

John Henry

Champion Hutton

One of my most memorable matches was when Hull beat Halifax in the 1956 Championship final at Maine Road, Manchester, with Colin Hutton kicking the winning penalty from near touch towards the end of the game. I knew he was going to kick that goal. I'd have bet money on it, such was the euphoria. People were turning away, covering their faces. But somehow I knew he would kick it. I felt it. I remember Halifax had a big coloured lad, Johnny Freeman, and coming out of the ground a friend and I were saying what a good player he was. We said with his speed, he could set the world alight. Unfortunately, two young ladies misunderstood us and thought we were being racist and we had to run for our lives. I also remember the Hull and Halifax Yorkshire Cup finals in the 1950s. They were real battles and fights broke out at the

scrums. And I remember Cyril Sykes getting injured in a championship final against Oldham and the referee penalised him for not getting up. Ganley kicked the goal and that turned the game and we lost. It's funny – I can remember matches all those years ago, but I can't remember what I had for breakfast this morning.

Ernie Mason

Everybody went Berserk

I remember going to Manchester as a kid with my dad and all his mates for the top four championship final against Halifax. Hutton kicked the winning goal and everybody went berserk. My dad had skimmed off work to go and I think he got sacked from BOCM for it. But he must have thought it was worth it. Another match that sticks out later on when I was a young man, was at Boothferry Park when we played Barrow in the top four play-off. I remember a Barrow forward, Jack Grundy, had his sleeves rolled right up to his shoulders virtually. We gave 'em a right good towsing because they were at Wembley the following week. There was always a big furore about whether they should play at Boothferry Park because it was a soccer ground and the Football League weren't too keen on it. But I saw Hull play Rovers there a number of times. We used to get a train to the ground from Stepney Lane when we lived on Beverley Road. I remember another semi-final against Oldham at Swinton and Bernard Ganley, Oldham's full-back, running amok. He literally jumped over a player. I can remember when Hull and Halifax played Carcassonne and Albi in the European Cup. In fact, we're still the holders of that trophy because I don't think they played for it again. I'll never forget one of Hull's players stamping on the head of this French hooker and the other Hull players started on their own man for doing it. One of the worst things I've seen on a rugby field was when Wakefield's Rocky Turner hit Peter Bateson in the championship semi-final. It was so blatant. The touch judges saw it, the referee saw it and nobody did a thing about it. They went out to kill us, because they were playing us at Wembley the following week. Then Tommy Harris got well done in the final.

RUGBY LEAGUE FOOTBALL
★
INTERNATIONAL
CLUB
CHAMPIONSHIP

HULL
English R.L. Champions, 1955/6
VERSUS
ALBI
French R.L. Champions, 1955/6

Souvenir
Programme 3d.

The 'International Club Championship', as stated on the programme, was better known as the European Club Championship and involved Hull, Halifax, Albi and Carcassonne. Hull won the 1956/57 tournament.

I remember us winning the Yorkshire Cup at Leeds. I had just started knocking around with our lass. She was still at school but I married her in the end. We went in the clubhouse with my dad and drank champagne out of the cup. I couldn't believe it. It was brilliant. And I remember winning the Floodlit Trophy, beating Rovers at The Boulevard. Manna from Heaven that was. It's another trophy nobody has ever took off us because they never played for it again. It's ours. If you want a tackle of all time, then it was against Widnes in the semi-final at Swinton. I remember Hogan making a break for Widnes and I think it was Ronnie Wileman who went after him and chopped him down on the twenty-five yard line. Bah, he didn't half give him one and we went on to Wembley.

Mike Adamson

Premature Celebrations

I have very fond memories of the game they won at Huddersfield to get promotion to Super League in 1997. Although if we had known then what was to follow it in the next two years, I don't know how many supporters would have celebrated it.

Keith Jenkinson

Vollenhoven Strikes Back

My first real collection of a big game was the semi-final at Odsal in 1961. It was against St Helens and Vollenhoven, their great winger, had said in the *Hull Daily Mail* that if Hull got to the final again it would be a bad thing for the game because

Magnificent late rally and glorious Bowman try earns Odsal replay

HULL 10   HALIFAX 10

HULL VERY NEARLY BEAT the Halifax hoodoo at Heading-ley this afternoon. Starting disappointingly, they warmed to their work in the second half, but it seemed as if Halifax would complete another Yorkshire Cup victory over Hull when Bowman dramatically took a quick toss from Moat and scored a glorious try in the corner to level the scores and make an Odsal replay necessary.

There were one or two incidents and Henderson, the Hali-fax forward, got his marching orders. Hull were well served by Finn and Moat and the pack, once again, did splendid things. Coverdale was by far the soundest tackler on the field.

By KINGSTONIAN

The Hull Daily Mail *reports the 1955 Yorkshire Cup final.*

they'd got two good hidings in the previous two. I remember at the match there was a Hull fan, he was absolutely stoned, with a bottle in each hand and he was waiting for Vollenhoven at the bottom of those longs steps where they came out at Odsal. He said he was going to get him and Vollenhoven had to walk down these steps with his back to the wall to keep out of the way of this guy. He was visibly shaken and the first pass he got, Terry Hollindrake came to tackle him. Hollindrake wasn't the most frightening of people, but Vollenhoven still threw the ball away as if he didn't want to know. But as the game went on, Vollenoven got better and I remember him going down the same stand side and waltzing around at least six Hull

players to score a brilliant try. We'd done all right until then, but once Vollenhoven got it that was it. One of the best tries I saw by a Hull player was scored by Keith Boxall. It was a John Player cup-tie against Leeds at The Boulevard in the Seventies. Boxall made this break down the middle and was faced by Syd Hynes, who was a bit of a hard case. He was the last line of defence and there was only him to stop Boxall, who was steaming at him. Boxall didn't try to side-step or swerve, but he literally ran through him and left Hynes on the grass in a crumpled heap and touched down under the sticks. Hull drew the game and we beat Leeds in the replay.

Steve Roberts

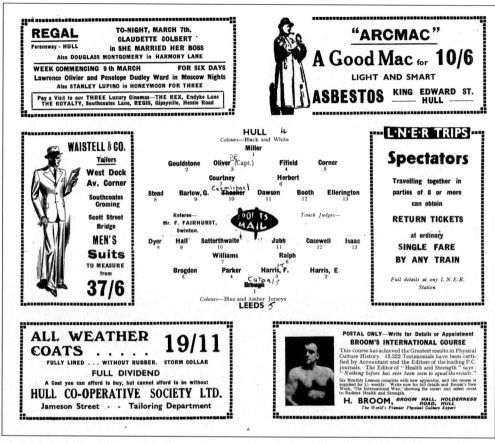

REGAL
Ferensway - HULL

TO-NIGHT, MARCH 7th.
CLAUDETTE COLBERT
in SHE MARRIED HER BOSS
Also DOUGLASS MONTGOMERY in HARMONY LANE

WEEK COMMENCING 9th MARCH   FOR SIX DAYS
Lawrence Olivier and Penelope Dudley Ward in Moscow Nights
Also STANLEY LUPINO in HONEYMOON FOR THREE

Pay a Visit to our THREE Luxury Cinemas—THE REX, Endyke Lane
THE ROYALTY, Southcoates Lane, REGIS, Gipsyville, Hessle Road

"ARCMAC"
A Good Mac for **10/6**
LIGHT AND SMART
ASBESTOS KING EDWARD ST. HULL

WAISTELL & CO.
Tailors
West Dock
Av. Corner
Southcoates
Crossing
Scott Street
Bridge
**MEN'S
Suits**
TO MEASURE from
37/6

·L·N·E·R· TRIPS·
Spectators
Travelling together in
parties of 8 or more
can obtain
RETURN TICKETS
at ordinary
**SINGLE FARE
BY ANY TRAIN**
Full details at any L.N.E.R.
Station

HULL 4
Colours—Black and White
Miller
1
Gouldstone 2   Oliver (Capt.) 3   Fifield 4   Corner 5
Courtney 7   Herbert 6
Stead 8   Barlow, G. 9   Carmichael / Thacker 10   Dawson 11   Booth 12   Ellerington 13

Referee—
Mr. F. FAIRHURST,
Swinton.

Touch Judges—

Dyer 8   Hall 9   Satterthwaite 10   Jubb 11   Casewell 12   Isaac 13
Williams 7   Ralph 6
Brogden 5   Parker 4   Harris, F. 3   Harris, E. 2
Caton / Brough
1
Colours—Blue and Amber Jerseys
LEEDS 5

**ALL WEATHER
COATS** **19/11**
FULLY LINED ... WITHOUT RUBBER. STORM COLLAR
FULL DIVIDEND
A Coat you can afford to buy, but cannot afford to be without
HULL CO-OPERATIVE SOCIETY LTD.
Jameson Street - - Tailoring Department

POSTAL ONLY—Write for Details or Appointment
BROOM'S INTERNATIONAL COURSE
This course has achieved the Greatest results in Physical
Culture History. 15,222 Testimonials have been certi-
fied by Accountant and the Editors of the leading P.C.
journals. The Editor of "Health and Strength" says :
"Nothing before has ever been seen to equal the results."
Six Monthly Lessons with new apparatus, and the course is
supplied for 1/- weekly. Write now for full details and Broom's New
Work, 'The International Way,' showing the surest and safest route
to Radient Health and Strength.
H. BROOM, BROOM HALL, HOLDERNESS
ROAD, HULL
The World's Premier Physical Culture Expert

The programme centre pages for the Hull v. Leeds third round RL Challenge Cup-tie in 1936, which drew a record Boulevard crowd of 28,798.

Let Off for Australia

The match which really stands out was a defeat, when we just lost to Australia in 1982. We scored a try right at the end and they disallowed it. If they'd had the video ref. then we'd have won. It happened right in front of us. We were stood on the hill and I thought we'd won. When the ref disallowed the try it was worse than losing at Wembley. They'd turned out their full Test side because they knew we were a good side. We would have been the only club side to have beaten them for years. Nobody will beat them now. But we

nearly did and that would have been something in history. One match I missed going to, which I still remember, was when they clinched promotion to Super League by beating Huddersfield. I watched it in Spain. I'd already booked the holiday and we were supposed to beat Featherstone to win the championship, but they beat us at home. So I was real disappointed, not knowing if Hull would get promoted. But when we got to Spain I found Sky TV were showing it. Me and my friend, Billy, went in this bar and asked if we could have the rugby on. They said 'Yes, it's on Saturday afternoon' I said 'No that's

Union, we want League at night'. Anyway, he let us and I can remember all these Spaniards looking at us and wondering 'what's this crazy man shouting at'. And I sang *Old Faithful* to them. It was a real good night. I've some of our big matches on video, like when we beat Widnes in the Premiership final and when it's a horrible day with nothing to do, I think I'll just cheer myself up and plug it in.

Dave Worsnop

Victory with Eleven Men

A game I remember was a murky, drizzly night in the early Seventies, Hull *v.* Leeds. We all hate Leeds. It was a Cup-tie and Leeds had Hynes, Atkinson, Smith, Shoebottom, Batten, Ramsey and all. Hull, with all due respect, were a bit of a mixture of misfits and a rabble. Leeds scored early and Hull hit back. Then bang. The idiot in the middle sends off one of Hull's ever so gentle forwards.

Brian Cooper makes a break in the 1959 Yorkshire Cup final against Featherstone Rovers.

Everybody in Threepennies thinks we've no chance now. Then with about ten minutes of the first half left, we watch in astonishment as the ref sends off Brian Hancock, Hull's captain and a player of impeccable character. This is too much for anyone and Jim Macklin says to the lads 'Come on' and the whole team start to walk off. As they near the tunnel the ref. tells Leeds to play on and Alf Macklin, the winger, shouts 'Come back lads they are playing on' and all the Hull team charges back. They're down to eleven men, but with ten minutes left Hull are still ahead. With the Threepennies going mad that remains the longest ten minutes of my life. Unbearable tension, throat sore as hell, no

Hull captain Dick Gemmell with the Yorkshire Cup after the defeat of Featherstone Rovers at Headingley in 1969.

nails and heart pounding. When the final whistle goes Hull's pack, Jim Macklin, bad Barry Kear and the rest fall to their knees shattered. We go ballistic and so ends, in my opinion, Hull FC's finest ever performance. Another memorable game came when Hull were being managed by a God-like figure called Brian Smith. He had transformed our team into a major force once more. He had made a silk purse out of a very tatty pig's ear. The venue was Central Park, Wigan, who were cock-a-hoop after winning the John Player Trophy and were on a fantastic winning run. We had gone from bottom to third in three months. Me and my mates positioned ourselves in the middle of a mass of pie-eaters and shouted ourselves hoarse as Hull started well, carried on well and finished well. Wigan's Edwards and Gregory were lost and Hanley lost his rag. It was a truly great night to be a black and white and my mate Mick Fisher stood on the bar in the Wigan club singing *Old Faithful*. Then there was the epic against the 1982 Australian touring team, the best team I have ever seen – apart from Hull, of course. On a freezing night I went straight to The Boulevard from work and waited outside for the gates to open and had a revolting cup of soup. I took my place on the '25', five steps up at the Airlie Street end in Threepenny Stand. It seemed to fill up in five minutes. By the time the teams ran out the atmosphere was electric. Within a few minutes Paul Rose took a swing at Ray Price, who ducked, and the game was on. It was rip-roaring stuff, Mick Harrison and the Aussie prop Young going at it like rutting stags. Toppo was trying his hardest to break down the Aussie defence and Hull led at half-time. Hull held out until about ten minutes from the full time with Mick Crane playing out of his skin, Crooks meeting fire with fire and all the lads battling like heroes.

Then Meninga came thundering down the Threepenny Stand side like a wild bull. Gary Kemble measured him and took him round the ankles with the best tackle I've ever seen. But as big Mal was going down he flicked the ball to the mighty figure of Eric 'The Guru' Grothe, who scored. Within five minutes Meninga came again exactly the same way, but when he saw Kemble blocking his way he kicked ahead and as these two great players raced after the ball the small figure of Tony Dean suddenly appeared out of nowhere, grabbed the ball, grinned and shot away. Great stuff. A final try by Grothe sealed it for Australia and as Meninga kicked the goal he ran back with his arm raised aloft as to say 'beat ya'. It was the only time I had seen this great man react to a crowd. Good on you, mate. What a game. What an atmospshere and what, even in defeat, a joy.

B.J. Knott

Floodlit Triumph

I remember when we played in the Floodlit Trophy final. That was brilliant because we beat Rovers. I can go back to the John Player final when we played Widnes and they beat us. But nobody had given us a chance anyway. We'd gone to Salford in the semi-final and we turned them over and Salford were a good team then.

Stephen Buckley

TV Thriller

A match that sticks out was the last game of the season in 1999. We were at the bottom of the table and playing Halifax at The

RUGBY LEAGUE
CHALLENGE CUP
Third Round

HULL
v.
WIGAN

Saturday, 19th March
ALL-TICKET MATCH

Prices.—Stand Seats (for seatholders only), 7/6; Ringside Seats, 5/-; East Stand, 4/6; West Stand. 3/6; North and South Terraces, 2/6.

Seatholders Only.—Seat tickets on sale at Secretary's Office from Tuesday to Friday this week, 10 a.m. to 5 p.m. daily, except Tuesday, when sale will continue to 6.30 p.m.

Other Passholders.—Tickets on sale to all other passholders at the above hours.

Open Sale.—Tickets will be on sale to all other supporters at the ground on SUNDAY, MARCH 13, at 9.30 a.m.

Advertisement for a 1960 Cup tie at The Boulevard.

Boulevard and Huddersfield were playing Castleford. It was either Hull or Huddersfield who were going to go down. The Huddersfield game was on Sky TV at the back of Threepenny Stand. Hull were winning, but we still needed Huddersfield to lose for us to stay up. It was just one of the most amazing days because of the tension watching both games. Castleford eventually ran away with it against Huddersfield and Hull won. Then everyone ran on to the pitch. Me and my friends got Michael Smith on our shoulders. I don't know why because he did bugger all and was quite a big player.

But that's how we felt. He was a hero for a day. Even when we lost to Huddersfield in the Divisional Premiership at Old Trafford, the whole atmosphere was amazing because once you get in a Hull group of supporters, everything just takes you away. It's weird. There's just something different about them. It's got no bearing to the outside world at all.

Craig Jessop

A Video Classic

One match I can remember really well is one I had on video for a long time until I lost it. It was at Barrow in the Cup and

Steve Norton took a pass from behind him. How he collected it I don't know. Then he went sixty yards, side-stepping around half a dozen players and gave it to that second row forward who always had a cig at half-time, Mick Crane, and he went over for the try. Fantastic. I'll always remember that. I used to sit and just watch that move on the video over and over again.

Peter Oglesby

Tremendous Leuluai

Some of the tries James Leuluai scored were tremendous, especially the one against

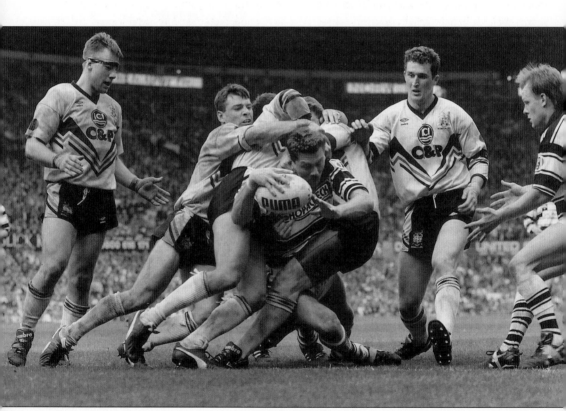

Gary Nolan squeezes through a massed Widnes defence to score the late try that clinched Hull victory in the 1991 Premiership Final – their last major trophy success.

Castleford in the Cup semi-final and the final against Wigan. They were brilliant and very similar tries. Another try that stands out was by Gary Nolan in the 1991 Premiership final defeat of Widnes. It wasn't a great try, but he scored it through a three-man tackle. We were right behind it and saw him bring his hand out and put the ball over the line. That was it. It won the match and brought us our first cup for a long while.

Rob Dale

Shared Enjoyment

The most enjoyable matches are the ones I shared with my son, Ben. Beating Wigan on a rain-soaked Tuesday night was one. Not only beating them, but stuffing them. Then there was the 1991 Premiership Final against Widnes at Old Trafford when we met an old work-mate, Tim, and his son. I remember all four of us went in a pub near the ground to find the place crammed full of Hull fans, many of them dressed in drag. That was one of the funniest moments.

Kevin Horsley

Super Sub Nolan

The 1991 Premiership Final is my favourite memory. In the quarter-final, we stuffed St Helens and faced big-spending Leeds in the semi at The Boulevard. It was all square in the last minute when Greg Mackey put an 'up and under' to Leeds' ex-All Black full-back John Gallagher, who knocked on over his own line for super sub Gary Nolan to score the winning try. The final was amazing. We had a great team of

hard-working players against the Widnes professionals. Martin Offiah didn't get a look in apart from when he ran the full length of the field only to be bundled into touch by Paul Eastwood centimetres from the line. In the second half Hull began to tire, but they held out superbly and up stepped Gary Nolan again to seal the game with another great try. The pop world had the Nolan sisters, but we had the Nolan brothers, Gary and Rob. Another game I remember was one Sunday afternoon, when Hull played champions Wigan at The Boulevard. That day I was playing in a tournament at The Cricket Circle across the road from The Boulevard. I was praying we wouldn't reach the final, otherwise I'd have missed the Hull game. Luckily, we lost in the semis and I managed to see Hull win 20-4 against a star-studded side. A recent memory is when we beat Wigan 14-4 in the Challenge Cup at home. It was the first time I had seen our new team. Everybody had written them off against Wigan. My friends at university said Hull had no chance, but I knew we would do it and we did – live on BBC TV.

Ben Horsley

Christening Highlight

I remember Gary Nolan scoring that last minute try against Leeds at The Boulevard in the 1991 Premiership semi-final. He took it out of Gallagher's hands. It was brilliant. The only thing is that I couldn't go to the final because I'd already agreed to go to a christening. After the christening we went back to the reception and ended up watching the match on TV and Gary Nolan did the same thing again. People kept popping in from the reception and wondering what the heck I was shouting about. The best atmosphere was when we clinched the Division One championship by winning at Huddersfield a couple of seasons ago. When you walked into the ground you could feel the tension and atmosphere. I'd never felt anything like it before. It was more like a home game because Hull fans filled one stand. You knew something was going to happen that day. It was special. The match that upset me more than any other was when they played Wigan at The Boulevard in a cup-tie. We were winning something like 21-6 at half time and we lost 22-21. It was unbelievable. Wigan hadn't lost a cup-tie for many years and we were the only team to get close. It was crazy. I thought we had it in the bag, we were that far ahead. It was shattering. We were robbed. We got pulled back to retake a penalty with their tryline begging. I thought that was a disgrace by the referee because when we took the penalty they were all diddling and one bloke was just getting onside. A try I remember is one I didn't see. Chico Jackson scored it against Featherstone. It was a right foggy day. Somebody scored a try and I didn't know who it was. All we heard was the referee blow the whistle for it and everybody was cheering for some reason. It turned out Chico Jackson had scored. A try that I did see and remember was one by Steve Prescott when he caught it under his own sticks and went the full length of the field. I think it was against Castleford. In the paper it said he ran ninety-five yards and I always thought from one set of sticks to the other was a hundred yards.

Graham Foot

Fantastic Atmosphere

The game that always stands out for me was not a final but a semi-final replay at Headingley against Castleford in 1985. The match was very physical and a fight broke out right on half-time when Cas's Mal Reilly had a go at Peter Sterling. It got the crowd psyched up and the atmosphere from the Hull fans, who were all in the South Stand, was fantastic – the best I've ever known. Great tries? The Ronnie Wileman try against Rovers at Headingley. I don't remember much about the match except the try. He just went down the touchline and nobody could catch him. You thought he must get caught, but he never did.

John Atkinson

Wileman replay

There's one try that I certainly won't forget – Ronnie Wileman's at Headingley against Rovers. From the halfway line on the outside he goes to acting half-back, picks up the ball and sets off fifty yards to the line down the wing. For some time after that the group I was with would re-enact it in a pub car-park or somewhere. We'd shout 'Ronnie Wileman' and that was the call for somebody to go to acting half-back before setting off looking as ponderous as possible. Another of us would do the TV commentary: 'It's Ronnie Wileman, Ronnie Wileman, Ronnie Wileman' over and over again. Another that stands out came in an electric match that was unbelievable. It was against the 1982 Kangaroos with David Topliss scoring just before half-time. He put in a little kick, followed up and disappeared under a whole mound of Australian bodies.

stralian injury blow on record night

ate burst foils ighting Hull

strolians 13

By RAYMOND FLETCHER

AUSTRALIANS a record-breaking ccessive win at the ard last night but ook most of the

led for over an efore the Austra-roduced their usual ul finish to register n that gave them longest winning ce by a touring

without Stone, tt and Norton pack rose to the n against the full of the Australian de with a battling in the loose and ear to extending wn winning run of atches.
ralia's gamble of g the full side four before Saturday's Wigan could have hem dearly for

Brentnall, the full back, suffered severe concussion and is doubtful.

Another casualty in a hectic battle was Hull centre Leuluai, who received a broken jaw.

And former Test hooker Bridges produced

an all-important 13-5 success in the scrums.

He was aided by another Test veteran in open side prop Harrison, making his first appearance for Hull since his return from Leeds.

In the absence of Norton, Crane took over at loose forward to win

Hull's man-of-the-match award.

Crane lost nothing in comparison with Price, the Australian No. 13 as he varied his tactics intelligently and was always a danger with his probing runs.

Crooks, dropped from the first test team, was also well to the fore with Rose revealing some of his old international form up front.

Behind them Topliss and Dean at half back worried the tourists with their tantalising play.

Topliss joined the elite band of six players who have scored a try against the Australians with a clever piece of football just before half time.

Sterling, the Australian scrum half took their man-of-the-match award

with a busy display and a hand in their first try.

After a wild first half tempers cooled down and penalties finished at 14-14.

The fiery start began with fists flying from both sides. Crooks and Boyd seemed to be trying to settle personal scores as their clashes led to others joining in.

Earlier Crooks had been penalised for an incident that left Krilich lying on the ground.

Rose showed how to inflict damage the proper way as the Hull forward bounded Boyd out of the way with a hefty but fair shoulder charge.

In between all the wild goings on the Australians twice narrowly missed taking the lead.

Yorkshire Post *report on Hull v. Australia in 1982.*

A frozen Boothferry Park is the venue for Hull's John Player Trophy semi-final clash with Leeds in 1985. David Topliss is the Hull player on the attack.

There is another try that sticks out. It was in the Challenge Cup at Warrington and Hull fans filled the railway end. It was scored by Phil Edmonds, who is somebody most people wouldn't recall. In fact, we used to laugh at him because he looked a bit like the Michelin man and became something of a favourite with us. It was a very close game – with minutes to go Hull are attacking the railway end and near the posts, when our hero of the moment, who didn't really damage many defences, came bursting onto this ball and scored right in front of all the Hull fans. That won the game and the crowd just went barmy jumping up and down. Then my specs flew off and landed on the terrace. So while everybody is going barmy, I'm on my hands and knees looking for my specs and shouting 'Mind my specs'. One of my first really important memories is when Hull won the Yorkshire Cup in 1969. We were living down south then, but we came up for the final at Headingley. I was nine and I can remember standing in what was then a well in the best stand. At the end of the game there was a benign pitch invasion and people chanting for Arthur Keegan, who was a big hero at the time but didn't play in the final because of injury.

Trevor Gibbons

Length of Field Match-winner

I saw a great try when I couldn't get into Threepennies because I got there late and I had to stand at the scoreboard end. It was against Wigan and I've a feeling Henderson Gill was on the wing for them and he'd been doing a bit of taunting after scoring relatively late on. There was no time left and I think the scores were tied or we might have been slightly behind and Joe Lydon went for a penalty goal from almost half-way. So if he kicked it or the ball went dead, Wigan had won. But it fell short and Gary Pearce made a breakthrough and then McCaffrey went all the way to the sticks. The hooter went as he put the ball down and the elation was fantastic. Winning the Premiership in 1991 was far more exciting than when we were winning cups in the Eighties. I'd only known success in the first few years of watching Hull and you can only really appreciate the good times if you've been through the bad. We had a few bad years in the Eighties, so winning the Premiership was great. It was so unexpected because Widnes had the likes of Martin Offiah and you thought we were just going there to make the numbers up. So when we won I was ecstatic. The players came over and sang *Old Faithful* to a packed Stretford end. My wife was with me, she didn't go to many matches, but she was there and was completely unmoved. I couldn't understand that because I thought it was the ultimate. Funnily enough, when we dropped into the Second Division and went to places like Dewsbury and Batley's inappropriately named Mount Pleasant, where the crowds were quite small, she got hooked on it. I think it was the humour on the terraces at the smaller grounds that did it rather than the big

Yorkshire Cup final ticket, 1986.

Keith Boxall makes a typical charge against Bradford Northern in 1981.

glamour occasions. She's a season-ticket holder herself now.

Ian Roberts

Advertised Try

One incident that really stands out for me was in a game they played at Leigh. I think Hull were losing 7-0 and Leigh's John Woods put in a kick from about forty metres out that hit the advertising hoarding near us behind the posts. The ball bounced back into the in-goal and he ran up and put his hand on it and the referee, who was way behind play, awarded a try. There was a near riot by Hull supporters massed at that end. Woods kicked the goal to make it 13-0, but Hull came back and I think we won 14-13. Another good memory is when we took a mini-bus to see Hull beat Widnes in the Premiership Final at Old Trafford. We got a puncture on the way

back, but we didn't care because Hull had won and we'd all had that much to drink. There was the driver trying to fix the spare wheel and nobody else was bothered. There were twelve of us, all mates together, decked out in black and white just having a good laugh and singing *Old Faithful*. It's all about comradeship. But it's the same even when we lose. We're still singing and dancing.

Mike Poole

Side-stepped Stretcher

I remember Dane O'Hara scoring a length of the field try for Hull at Castleford. One of the Hull players got injured and the stretcher-bearers came on and they almost injured two other players when they ran on to the pitch. O'Hara had to do a side-step round the stretcher to score the try. Then when they were carrying the Hull player on the stretcher he fell off.

Bob Cone

Matches Remembered a Lifetime

There have been so many great matches and some are now just fading memories. I remember there was a Yorkshire Cup-tie against Huddersfield in the 1950s that I regarded as the greatest game I'd ever seen. But I was only a young teenager then and didn't have so many to compare it with. It still stands out though. It was a midweek match and I went straight from school. Huddersfield still had a lot of respect then and looked magnificent in their claret and gold jerseys. The great Lionel Cooper was playing for them

and I've got a feeling a young Mick Sullivan was also in the team. Hull were just emerging as an outstanding team with Johnny Whiteley one of several promising young players. I can't remember any details about the match but retain an overall impression that it was special and Hull won quite comfortably in the end. I also remember the *Hull Daily Mail* saying that this was one of the best games seen at The Boulevard for years. A year or two later there was a game against York which Hull won by about 40 points. It obviously wasn't a great game, but I remember Hull playing almost perfect rugby and rating it the best performance I had seen at that time. Again I can't recall details but retain an overall impression of it being an incredible exhibition of all-out attacking rugby. It was just a great team display although I think somebody scored four tries, probably Carl Turner or

Carl Turner flips a back pass to Brian Cooper against Leeds at Headingley in 1956. Keith Bowman is in support.

Paul Prendiville cuts inside against Featherstone Rovers in 1983. Barry Banks (left) and David Topliss are close by.

Tommy Finn. This was another game that the *Hull Daily Mail* went overboard on. I wonder how many others remember it now.

Charles Arnold

Rip-roaring Cup-tie

A match that readily comes to mind when talking about great games is the Hull *v.* Castleford semi-final replay in 1985. It was a good game from first to last, but it's the first forty minutes that stand out. Even now I think of it as the most intense, fierce and breathtaking forty minutes I've ever seen. It was fast and furious and, let's be honest, brutal. It had everything. Great passing movements, thrilling chases and a brawl. Peter Sterling was irrepressible that night and Cas did all they could to stop him. Hull won the game in the first half and did well to hold back Cas in the second. But Gary Kemble suffered bad

concussion from a late tackle and I think that could have cost Hull the Cup because he wasn't the same at Wembley and at his best would probably have stopped at least two of the Wigan tries. Going much further back there was the 1958 Championship semi-final at Oldham. Oldham had a great team then, but Hull's pack tore them apart. I think it was played on a Saturday evening for some reason, probably because the FA Cup was on TV in the afternoon. The pitch was a typical end of season dust bowl, which you used to get then. Hull's forwards just bounced the Oldham lot all round it. I think Hull won by about 20 points even though Tommy Harris was sent off for flattening their scrum-half Frank Pitchford. I think Oldham had finished at top and Hull were fourth but they became champions by beating Workington in the final. I remember them coming home with the trophy along a packed Hessle Road.

Ray Ford

CHAPTER 4
Wembley Heartbreak and Elland Road Delight

The Duke of Edinburgh talks to Tongan centre Nanumi Halafihi before the 1960 Cup Final at Wembley.

Sir Tom Courtenay Remembers

From my point of view, Dad's keenly anticipated trip to Wembley was very badly timed. I had been prevailed upon to appear, on the evening of the match, with some former university friends in a performance of Chekhov one-act plays at Senate House, London University's Union. It was just across the street from RADA's Vanbrugh Theatre. This is why Mother had been reading Chekhov. I was the nervous young man in *The Proposal*, and I also performed a monologue, *The Harmfulness of Tobacco*. So

Actor Tom Courtenay and his father, wearing Hull rosettes, ready for Wembley in 1959. (Photograph from Sir Tom Courtenay's collection.)

I had plenty on that day. There's a photo of Dad and me on his great day out. He looks as though he's had a couple and I look like I want to be a million miles away. In fact, I left shortly after half-time. Hull were getting hammered and lost to Wigan by a record score. I can see the mighty Billy Boston flying towards the Hull line, knocking over anyone in his path. So no *Old Faithful* sung to celebrate victory. Dad, I'm sure, would have bumped into plenty of Hull supporters after the game, with whom he could commiserate and reflect on the thrill of Wembley. I had to go and perform. Quote from my pocket diary, Saturday 9 May 1959: *Met Dad, went to Wembley. Played Chekhov in evening. Quite a day.*

Sir Tom Courtenay

Winning at Wembley is Everything

When you talk to Hull supporters of my era and ask them 'What would you rather do, win the Cup at Wembley or the Grand Final at Old Trafford?' I'm sure to a man they would opt for winning at Wembley. Hull's never done it. That's why we've always been chided by the opposition, especially Rovers fans. You know, singing 'You'll never win at Wembley'. Losing to Wigan 28-24 was bad enough. They said it was the best ever final, but if we'd won 1-0 in a poor game that would have done me. The Featherstone final was the hardest to take. We all thought, this is the one when we're going to do it. Now we'll show everybody. We were big favourites. But we lost and to see grown men, myself included, crying at the end was awful. I said then that if we ever win at Wembley they are never going to get me out of the place. I would chain myself in and they would have to saw them off to get me out. I'd just want to stay there and enjoy the occasion as long as possible. I cannot look back on any of Hull's trips to Wembley and say I really enjoyed the day out. Funnily enough, the one I enjoyed a little bit was the one I should have enjoyed least. That was when we played Rovers. I don't know why. Perhaps it was the occasion that made it special.

Steve Roberts

The Fred Lindop Final

My worst rugby memory is the 1980 Wembley final. I'd never been to Wembley, but in the September of that season, my dad said we're going to Wembley whatever and fortunately Hull got there. I'll never forget Roger Millward lifting that Cup for Hull KR. It broke my heart as a twelve-year-old boy. I remember coming out of the ground crying my eyes out and some woman coming up to me and giving me fifty pence. She said: 'Don't worry love I'm from Batley and we'll never get to Wembley.' The 1980 final is known as the 'Fred Lindop Final'. I always remember the big banner when Hull came back from Wembley which said 'Lindop 10 Hull 5'. I've got the match on video when Lindop disallowed two tries but I don't watch it very often. I'd rather have not been there at all. The following day, Sunday, we were going away with school for a week. I'd never been away from home before and just didn't want to go. The 1983 14-12 defeat by Featherstone was the other heartbreaker when Charlie Stone butted one of their players and they kicked the winning penalty. When the ball went over

there was a sense of shock. We were numbed because in the 1985 final we knew it would be much more difficult against Wigan. But in 1983, as far as I was concerned there was only going to be one team that would win it and that was Hull. That was the hardest defeat to take. The 1982 Cup replay at Elland Road is my best highlight. I've never seen a night like that. I've been in some large football stadiums and Wembley with 100,000 there, but that night at Elland Road will never be forgotten by anyone who was there. The atmosphere was fantastic. I was twelve and that afternoon I left school early, telling them I was going to the dentist or something like that. There were three or four others lads leaving and my PE teacher. Coming back on the M62 with people waving their flags and tooting their horns was fantastic.

Simon Shaw

Devastated

I remember being devastated when they lost to Featherstone at Wembley. I mean, we went there expecting to win. It was terrible. Even the Featherstone fans we met on the tube after the match said they couldn't believe they'd won. They just did not expect to win. That didn't help how I felt. It had been different the year before when we won the Cup in the replay at Elland Road. The atmosphere then was unbelievable. I can see Crooks now lifting that Cup up. Then coming back to Hull and seeing them outside the City Hall with the Cup. That was a good time.

Dave Worsnop

Featherstone Final the Worst

I remember the trips to Wembley in the Eighties and the biggest disappointment was losing to Featherstone. I think all the supporters and probably the team were a bit complacent. It was probably even more disappointing than losing to Rovers in 1980, I would say. The Featherstone game was the worst because Hull just played so badly. Even then they got into the position to be leading 12-5 and still managed to throw the game away. Hull K.R. fans would probably say different but I think we should have beaten them as well. I remember we had one or two tries disallowed for forward passes for Graham

Bray and Keith Tindall. The second half of the game seemed to be over in ten minutes although to Rovers fans it must have seemed like an hour as Hull fought back. I was disappointed, but not to the extent that it really upset me. I saw all four of the finals when Hull got to Wembley in the Eighties and they never did themselves justice in any. The Rovers game they should have won but didn't. I also remember the semi-final that year when Hull got to Wembley for the first time while I'd been watching them. They played Widnes at Swinton and at that time I'd never really seen them win anything and had certainly never been to Wembley. I was very ecstatic and we had a great celebration

A typical group of Hull fans about to set off for Wembley in 1959.

Johnny Whiteley leads Hull's team out to meet Wigan at Wembley in 1959.

after that. Against Widnes at Wembley they did well to come back and I remember being stood at one end of the ground when Stuart Wright was running down the field towards me after intercepting and I thought 'That's it, it's gone now' but Hull came back with two tries to draw. Everybody talks about the final against Wigan in 1985 being a great game and to neutrals I imagine it was. They were two good, probably great, sides, although Hull were just going a bit then. They got off to such a good start and scored a try. Then from a Hull fan's point of view they let Wigan get in front and by the time they came back it was too late. So my overall memories of Wembley are of disappointment. But

winning the Cup at Elland Road made up for it. In some respects it was as good an atmosphere as Wembley in a slightly different way and it didn't take anything away from it for me. If you look at Wembley in the cold light of day it was probably due to be pulled down anyway.

Keith Jenkinson

Costly Goal Misses

The Wembley matches were hard to take. The one against Rovers – God, that was heartbreaking. But the worst was the one against Featherstone. I had it in my head that Hull just had to turn up and do the business, but Featherstone turned us over. Sammy Lloyd missed with a couple of goal-kicks that he would normally have kicked with his slippers on. That was bad to take. I was so down after the game. I wish we could have won at Wembley and even a draw against Widnes I thought was such an achievement. But winning the Cup at Elland Road made up for it. It didn't matter it wasn't at Wembley. It was having our name on the Challenge Cup that mattered and I was there to see it. But one

match that really stands out is the Challenge Cup semi-final against Widnes in 1980 when we beat them 10-5 after Wileman went over in the last minute, I think. Sammy Lloyd kicked a goal off the touchline. It was a stormer. That was the turning point for the club. We just went on from there.

Stephen Buckley

1980 Wembley ticket for Hull v. Hull Kingston Rovers.

What a Night!

I don't like to think about the Wembley finals and the match which gave myself and all my mates the biggest thrill, buzz and utter pride was the Challenge Cup final replay against Widnes at Elland Road in 1982. We hired a minibus and driver for the journey from Hull to Leeds and what a great job he did dodging all the horrendous traffic jams. People were still arriving at half-time, but we got there in good time. I met my brother Paul, who was coming from Manchester, outside the old Greyhound Stadium and we joined the lads on the Kop end. After a couple of scares from Andy Gregory and Mick Adams, enter Toppo (Topliss), Jimmy (Leuluai) and Gary (Kemble) with the two most delicious runarounds you ever did see. And two of the best tries you ever did see. With Knocker Norton running as only he could, Dukes shovelling the ball out and Sully – a great, great man – looking on out on the wing, Hull were on top. Then Toppo reached out in front of us for a try and finally Crooks surged under the sticks. 'Bloody hell,' said my mate Bill. 'We've won the Cup'. I kissed our kid and when I got back to the minibus, the look of pride on Dad's face was such a joy. He had been born in the year Hull had last won the Cup, 1914. There were handshakes, hugs and kisses all round. Then off to the pub. Colin knew this pub in Leeds. 'Turn the telly on, missus,' said George as we entered. She looked on at this mini invasion with trepidation but went along with his request. What a night, what a party. The landlady, bless her, called a lock-in for all the fans, Hull, Leeds, Hunslet and even some from Widnes. We left for Hull at about one o'clock singing *Old Faithful* for about the 150th time.

B.J. Knott

All Hull Let Loose

I remember Hull playing Rovers at Wembley and the headline 'All Hull let loose'. It was a fantastic occasion for the city of Hull. I know we got beat but both sides earned credit. We went down on Bluebird coaches as we did all the away matches. The Featherstone final at Wembley knocked us all to bits because on paper we just couldn't lose. We had Fred Ah Kui, Leuluai, Knocker Norton. It was a case of how many points we would put past them. That was the game that upset me most. Winning the Cup against Widnes at Elland Road was special. It didn't matter that it wasn't at Wembley. Just winning the Cup was enough. I'd still like Hull to win at Wembley, of course. But it might not be the same now that they've changed Wembley. It's gone now.

Ian Anderson

Killer penalty

I remember the 1960 Wembley final against Wakefield. I saw that on television. Hull had a lot of injuries and one player played with an injured head. The loss to Featherstone at Wembley was hard to take. I remember there was an ex-Featherstone player playing for Hull, Charlie Stone I think it was, and he flattened a Featherstone player right under the posts with a few minutes to go. They kicked the penalty and won the game. I always said deep down he was a Featherstone supporter.

Peter Oglesby

Fantastic Game

My first real memory of watching Hull is the 1980 final at Wembley against Rovers when I was eight. In fact, I don't remember much about the game, but I do know I wore a big black and white hat. I went with my parents and it was the occasion rather than the match which I remember. But I do remember the 1985 Wembley final very well when we lost to Wigan. I went on a school trip. It was just a fantastic game, probably the best I've ever seen. It was a match of extremes. We were pretty depressed when Hull were getting well beaten at one stage. Then they came back and we thought they might do it in the end. It was such a good game and Hull played so well I wasn't really bothered that they got beaten. The 1983 final was the worst because we were expected to win. We were so confident we were going to break our Wembley jinx. I was pretty sick about it, although I don't remember much detail. I think I've tried to forget about that one. A good memory was Hull winning the Cup in the replay against Widnes. I remember losing my programme when Lee Crooks scored. I threw it in the air and it got lost in the vast amount of Hulls fans there. I think I was in tears at one point that night. It meant that much to me even at that tender age. I was eleven.

Rob Dale

Charlie Birdsall sets up an attack against Hull Kingston Rovers at Wembley in 1980.

City Closed Down

I went with school to watch Hull and Rovers at Wembley and I remember that the city of Hull closed down. Rovers won, so one half of the city was smiling and the other half wasn't. I can't tell you how bad it affected me. We've never lived it down to this day. I think Rovers still have a club room called 10-5, which was the result. I'm not sure because I never go near the place unless Hull are playing there. I'd sooner set my head on fire. I saw Hull lose at Wembley a few times and I saw them draw against Widnes. I remember I was behind the posts when Sammy Lloyd had that late kick at goal. It was sailing over and then it just blew to one side and they drew. I didn't see them when they won the Cup in the replay because I was at home doing my homework. I listened to the match on the radio and we were going mad. It was absolutely brilliant. Although I wasn't there it was still one of my best memories.

David Boast

I Thought I'd Died

The first time I saw Hull at Wembley was against Rovers in 1980. The match itself is a blur. I booked my ticket before the first round, but I don't remember much about the game, apart from Roger Millward getting injured. The thing I remember most is afterwards, singing and dancing in the coach and looking across and seeing some of the Rovers fans, who looked as if they had just lost. We were out to enjoy the occasion and we did. It was a good atmosphere. But to be beaten by Featherstone at Wembley … I thought I'd

1980 Wembley programme.

died. I actually left everybody and went back to the coach, sat down and cried. It was that bad. Everybody was the same. Nobody could believe we got beat. I mean Featherstone? We thought we could beat them stood on our hands. We just didn't perform. The Wigan Wembley final was such a mixture of emotions. I remember thinking at one time, that's it we've had it. A kid took his shirt off and threw it away at half-time. But by the end of the match everybody was going crazy thinking we were going to win it. We didn't, but it didn't bother me too much because the players had really tried. One of the worst disappointments was when we drew against Widnes at Wembley. It was an odd feeling.

Steve Norton finds his way blocked in the 1980 Wembley final against Hull Kingston Rovers.

You didn't know how to feel because you had to go through it all again. It was flat. Normally you go to Wembley and one team's going crazy and the other's sat there miserable. But after the Widnes game everybody was flat. Winning the replay was brilliant. That was one of the most memorable matches. We'd done it, finally won the Challenge Cup. The atmosphere was great. We were packed tight, but still bouncing about after we'd won it.

Andy Scarah

It Still Hurts

I remember all the Wembley finals Hull were in, especially when we lost to Rovers. We wasn't allowed to forget because their supporters used to have the score in their bedroom windows for ages. But when we left Wembley you would have thought we'd won because we were cheering and Rovers supporters looked so miserable. They had faces like wet leeks. But we always cheer the side at the end, whether they play well or not, apart from an element who boo and carry on because I don't think they understand rugby league. I remember winning the Cup at Elland Road, but it was a shame it wasn't at Wembley. They still let us know that we can't win at Wembley. That hurts.

Doreen Scarah

Going to Wembley in Style

For the 1980 Cup Final against Rovers, a group of us borrowed a massive white Mercedes from a garage in Hull. We decorated it with black and white tape from the badge up the bonnet to the front windows like a wedding car. Two things went wrong that day. Firstly, Hull lost 10-5 and secondly the car broke down at Watford on the way home. While waiting at the service station a low loader arrived to take us home, so we popped open a bottle of champagne and began chanting 'We lost the Cup' to the amazement of everybody. They didn't understand the Hull FC humour. But the final memory of that night is still of a big Mercs. decorated like a wedding car being towed up the M1 on the back of a lorry. The atmosphere was electric that day, yet so friendly. The media wanted to create trouble, but to the credit of both sets of supporters a carnival atmosphere was created with couples and families walking down Wembley Way with mixed allegiances. I will never forget the

Dane O'Hara dives over for the equalising try that earned Hull a Challenge Cup final replay against Widnes in 1982.

Lee Crooks scores the late try that clinched Hull victory in the 1982 replay to bring the Cup back to Hull for the first time since 1914.

sign that covered the fish shop on Boothferry Road: 'Will the last one out please turn off the lights'. The thing I remember about Hull's 14-14 draw with Widnes at Wembley was a strange silence and feeling when the match finished. Both sets of fans stood with mouths open, not sure what would happen next. But the replay was fantastic. It was the right result and a black and white Challenge Cup winners' medal for the greatest ambassador the game has seen – Clive Sullivan.

Kevin Horsley

Rovers Won't Let Us Forget

A bad memory was when Rovers beat us at Wembley. We went with a trip from the pub where my brother-in-law used to be landlord. I hate Rovers, but the couple we were with were Rovers supporters. Oh dear me. They gave us some stick, but it was in fun. Rovers supporters still won't let us forget it. It's the only thing they've got left. The match I remember most was when we beat Widnes in the replay after Wembley. Widnes were so cocky. They just had to turn up to win and we beat them. That was heart-stopping for me. It's funny, but I don't remember all that much about the game because I was so emotional. We'd won and I seemed to forget everything else. Winning was the thing. I remember going there and thinking we hadn't a chance. I didn't go to the Wembley final because I was racing my pigeons.

Barry Scarah

On Guard Duty

I was in the army when Hull got to Wembley, so I couldn't go but I watched them on telly. Every time they got to Wembley I put a five pound bet on them and always ended up paying out. I was in Ireland with the army when Hull played Wigan at Wembley in 1985. And for the final against Widnes I had a ticket for Wembley that my granddad got me, but I couldn't go because I was on guard duty. I tried to sell my guard, but nobody would buy it off me. I saw it on the telly with another bloke, who wasn't actually a rugby league fan but watched it because he wanted to take five quid off me. I missed the match when they won the Cup in the replay and I've never seen them actually lift the Challenge Cup. I live for that day.

Graham Foot

Thought We Couldn't Lose

The biggest Wembley disappointment was when they lost to Featherstone. That was a nightmare. I remember on the way to Wembley we went by a betting shop that had Hull at 7-1 on to win the game. It wasn't worth having a bet, we just assumed Hull only had to turn up to win. But they didn't turn up. As the game went along I had a feeling they weren't going to win it. After only half an hour I thought it was going to be one of those days. Afterwards all the Hull fans were in total disbelief. I went to all the Wembley finals and the replay at Elland Road, but I nearly missed that. I went with my wife, her sister and my father-in-law by car. We all had tickets and we got to the ground at about 7 o'clock and was told that the ground was full. We were locked out. We showed them our tickets, but they said 'Sorry, it's absolutely jam-packed. We can't get anymore in'. The game kicked off and we were still outside. It got to about fifteen minutes into the game and Hull scored a try. We didn't have a radio with us, but gathered by the amount of noise coming out of the ground that it was Hull who had scored because Hull fans outnumbered Widnes's by quite a lot. It was really frustrating because we were glad they had scored, but fed up that we couldn't see it. We thought we would never get in. We were going to go back to the car and listen to it on the radio. Then one of the stewards came up to us and asked if we had tickets. We said we had standing tickets and he took us round the side, up some steps and we ended up on the back row at halfway in the best seats in the house. There had been other fans still milling about outside, but the steward just grabbed us four and took us to the seats.

John Atkinson

Longing for that Wembley Feeling

My dad took me to see Hull in four or five finals at Wembley, including the one against Hull Kingston Rovers. But I was so young I don't remember much about it apart from the walk up to Wembley Stadium itself. If I could ask for one thing to come back it would be to have that feeling again. I'd just love Hull to get back to Wembley, win or lose. It's just the atmosphere I'd like to experience again. Going down to London and seeing all the coaches on the motorway and things like that. I'd probably appreciate it more now

Topliss ends Hull's

Hull 18, Widnes 9

RUGBY LEAGUE

Raymond Fletcher

HULL have won the cup. After 68 years the old Northern Union trophy, now the RL Challenge Cup, is on its way back to the Boulevard for only the second time in its long history.

Before a crowd of nearly 40,000 packed into Elland Road they rose to the occasion magnificently in a tension-packed replay with every charge, every sweeping movement cheered to the echo by their delirious fans.

The roar was deafening as Topliss, Hull's captain stepped forward to receive the cup on the field from Mr. Neil Macfarlane, the Minister for Sport, with not a hint of trouble from the fans.

Widnes played their part in a magnificent spectacle but this was Hull's night. They put behind them the frustrations of Wembley and the disappointment of the Premiership thrashing by Widnes on Saturday and all hit top form together.

It was full justification to Arthur Bunting being named last week as the coach of the season. After recent setbacks Bunting did a magnificent job in restoring spirits and getting Hull back on the victory path.

Fittingly Topliss carried off the man-of-the-match award. The stand-off had often been fighting a lone battle in the two previous encounters and this time with greater support he rose to even greater heights.

Topliss scored two electrifying tries as he regained all his old speed to slice through the usually watertight Widnes defence.

Then Duke, playing in his first final at 37 after 15 years with Hull, gave Test hooker Elwell a 13-6 trouncing in the scrums.

That was the basis of Hull's victory. It allo Dean, another of over-30s, to produce performance Bunting looking for after lea him out of the Wem and Premiership clash

Although Gregory a superb game for Wi the youngster had to second place to Dea scrum-half honours.

Norton also rega the form that made player of the seasor leave no doubt that this night at least he far superior to Adams Widnes and Test riva loose-forward.

All the Hull forw deserved the hig praise but special men must be made of Crool

The 18-year-old sec row forward showed signs of nerves as landed three goals scored a clever solo that killed off Wic eight minutes from tin

Although Hull plenty of possession alties went hea against them 16-7, Burke keeping Widne

Pictures by BRUCE GREER TERRY CARROTT

touch with three goa make Hull's four tri one superiority look convincing.

Hull showed a wil ness to try something right from the start Prendiville field Widnes's kick-off hoisting a high ball which he followed u regather on the bou The tactical battle begun.

Widnes made the threatening raid Cunningham , pow hard down the left to with O'Loughlin be Basnett was brought by Kemble's flying t near the corner flag.

Hull respon superbly with No making a tremendous down the middle be losing his support. pressure was kept on Crooks failed with a yard drop goal effort.

With the el atmosphere increasir the time the sta seemed to be beco over-full and spect

Hull joy as Topliss scores his second try.

Left: David Topliss breaks through for his first try. Right: Lee Crooks scores.

Yorkshire Post *match report of the 1982 replay victory.*

68-year wait

spilled on to the field behind the Hull posts.

A loudspeaker announcement called for spectators to move forward as there were still many to come in 20 minutes after the kick-off.

They would not have seen the first score after Hull were unluckily caught offside. From just a yard inside Hull's half Burke landed a magnificent straight goal in the 18th minute.

A few minutes later he was off target with another shot followed soon after by a drop goal miss by Dean for Hull.

Duke was shovelling out the ball from the scrums for Hull as they hit Widnes with a series of midfield raids. Still the Widnes defence did not crack until two brilliant pieces of football split them wide open in the last seven minutes of the half.

Both came from well-planned and perfectly executed moves from scrums. The first followed a quick tap penalty with most of the Widnes pack not aware what was happening as the ball was cleared from the ruck.

Norton moved away with it before Kemble came tearing up from full-back to go away from the cover in a wide curving run for the touchdown.

Crooks added the goal in the 33rd minute and Hull were back four minutes later with another blinding try that baffled Widnes completely.

It was carried out at such speed that it was difficult to trace its movement. The only certainty is that Topliss was the scorer following the same path as Kemble.

Leuluai was also involved with Kemble being watched closely this time as he went away on a dummy run. Crooks failed with the kick but Hull could feel well satisfied with their 8-2 interval lead.

A run of seven penalties out of eight allowed Widnes to pile on the pressure and brought them a 57th minute goal from 20 yards by Burke.

A minute later Widnes were only a point behind as they went right back on

the attack with a brilliant kick and run raid by Gregory.

The scrum half was stopped by Kemble but Elwell moved the ball swiftly from acting half-back for O'Loughlin to send in the unmarked Wright at the corner.

Burke'sick from the touchline hit a post. This magnificent game then took another turn as Hull's forwards charged down the middle to set up Topliss's second try.

Norton drew the defence and Topliss went round him to take the pass and there was nothing going to stop him as he went hard for the line in the 62nd minute.

Crooks added the goal before Burke pulled back two points with another penalty for Widnes

For the moment it looked as if Widnes were going to pull off another of their amazing late escapes but Hull were not to be caught and Crooks made certain of victory as he went in for a try between the posts and added the goal.

HULL: Kemble; Sullivan, Leuluai, Evans, Prendiville, Topliss, Dean; Tindall, Duke, Stone, Skerrett, Crooks, Norton (Crane 74 mins).
WIDNES: Burke; Wright, O'Loughlin, Cunningham, Basnett, Hughes, Gregory; M. O'Neill, Elwell, Lockwood, Gorley, Prescott, Adams.
Referee: Mr. G. F. Lindop (Wakefield)

Dave Topliss holding the trophy, is hoisted on to the shoulders of team mates Keith Tindall, left, and Lee Crooks, watched by Gary Kemble.

My happiest moment

HULL'S captain David Topliss, scorer of two tries, said: "I've devoted my life to rugby league and this is the happiest moment I can remember.

"I went through four months of agony with my leg injury but tonight made it all worthwhile.

"The first try I got worked like a charm. We tried the move twice at Wembley but each time Eric Hughes spotted it and snuffed us out. But tonight the defence just opened up and I was over."

Lee Crooks, the 18-year-old forward who scored Hull's killer try nine minutes from time, admitted afterwards that his original intention had been to drop a goal.

"As I started to move

forward to get into position I saw a gap appear and I went for it. I was surprised how easily I got to the line.

"I always hoped I would be in a cup winning team some time in my career, but for it to happen when I'm only 18 is fantastic."

Arthur Bunting, Hull's manager, said: "We went to work on Saturday's defeat in the Premiership final and came up with all the right answers.

"I admit we squandered a bit of possession away but we were determined to play them at 13-man rugby to counter their defensive skills and it worked a treat because we scored four tries

"I was worried when they came back in the second half but we

showed great spirit when we countered so successfully in the final stages."

Doug Laughton, the Widnes coach, said: "I can have no complaints at the result. My side gave all they had

David Oxley, league secretary, paid a special tribute to the way Leeds United had handled the game

Chief Supt. Eric Walker said: "The crowd were wonderful. They were extremely well behaved. I only wish I had this sort of crowd to deal with every Saturday.

"The trouble was the colume of traffic from Hull descended on us very late and some spectators did not get in until half time but they took it all very well indeed."

Gary Kemble goes in for a vital try during the 1982 Challenge Cup replay against Widnes.

and I would be able to remember more about it.

Mark Donoghue

A Fan Is Born

It's no wonder my son Trevor became a Hull fan because he was born the weekend Hull played Wakefield at Wembley in 1960. I was obviously heavily pregnant on the Saturday and expecting any minute. But his dad still went to Wembley, as they did in those days, leaving me to it. You wouldn't get away with that these days. Even the players miss games because the wife's having a baby now. I still

kept an eye on the game on the telly, watching bits of it in some discomfort with my mother and the midwife popping in and out to keep an eye on me. But my husband had a great time at Wembley. Apparently he and his mates had decided that they would have a drink out of this hip flask every time Hull scored. The problem was Hull hardly scored, so they revised the plan during the game and decided to have a drink every time anybody scored. Well, Wakefield went on to win by a record score, so he'd downed plenty by the time the match finished. It took them longer to get back from London in those days, so he was coming home in the small hours of the morning somewhat the worse for wear. I only heard about all this later, but he was staggering up to our house in Anlaby Park Road and noticed the midwife's Mini or scooter parked outside. So she was already there. Trevor hadn't quite been born and as my husband came in the midwife took one look at him and said 'You had better get yourself to bed and sleep it off'. She guided him to a spare bedroom and he collapsed in an alcoholic haze. That's how Trevor was born, with his dad nursing a Wembley hangover. So Trevor was more or less a Hull fan from the day he was born. Another funny thing about it is that we found out many years later that Trevor's future wife Sheila's dad was also at the game – as a Wakefield supporter.

Shirley Gibbons

The Depths of Despair

Wembley has not had any happy memories for us Hull fans but the depths of despair was in 1980 because we lost to Rovers. And we still feel we was robbed, even if it maybe isn't true after watching the tape. You also felt for Sammy Lloyd because he was a great goal kicker normally, but he missed them when most needed. Yet those finals were something of an anti-climax because there was a big group of us, real Hull fans, who went everywhere to watch them. But when you went to Wembley you'd get a lot of people who didn't go all the time and they didn't really join in like the rest of us. We'd be stood on the hill, as you could at Wembley then, and we'd try to get *Old Faithful* going. But you'd suddenly find you were with a bunch of people who didn't really know the words of the song. I found that a bit depressing. But the worst bit of all was that 'Oh no, here we go again' feeling when it looked as if Hull were going lose another Cup final. I can remember after one final, it must have been 1985 when we lost to Wigan, and we were all sat on the steps outside the ground. My sister was more or less bursting into tears and I was near to tears trying to comfort her. There were others like us and you wonder why you put yourself through it. But in my case I'm thinking I want Hull to do it for my dad. He's seen all Hull's finals at Wembley and never seen them win. That's why when fans of other clubs start singing 'Old Faithful, you'll never win at Wembley' it does hurt. That's why they do it. I'd always assumed it would happen one day, and I'd just like to be there, with my dad. It would be one of the best days of my life. The feeling at the end of 1982 game, when we drew with Widnes, was in some ways even worse because it was like 'Well, what happens now?' It was an absolute anti-climax. So we've never had a great feeling after a Wembley final. Winning the Cup has always been a big thing with us. My granddad actually saw Hull win the Cup in 1914. When he was alive he used to tell me about it. Though he might get confused

Merry Christmas and a Happy New Year

Christmas card 1982. Santa Claus has the Challenge Cup in the bag for Hull.

about more modern things, he could you tell you clearly about the team Billy Batten was in that won the Cup. Sometimes, being quite young, I was only half listening but he would be off in his own world recalling players and matches of about sixty years earlier. So, I grew up quite aware of who Batten was and what Hull had done.

Trevor Gibbons

A Lovely Buffet

I went to two or three Wembleys to see Hull, but I didn't go to them all when they got there because I had two children. I wept a few tears when they lost, especially when they played Rovers. I was really upset then. But they still came back to the club, to a lovely buffet we did.

Ivy Mason

Arrested!

I once got arrested at Wembley with Percy Johnson, who had the Corn Exchange and was a Rovers' director. It was when Hull played Rovers and we bought a load of tickets from a bloke at Leeds. But when we got to Wembley we found they'd all been nicked out of Hunslet's club and we didn't know. The fans who had bought them off us started pointing us out at Wembley, saying 'There they are, that's them who sold us the ticket'. It turned out the guy who sold them to us was a gangster in Leeds, who'd broke into the Hunslet club. Great days. I saw all of Hull's Wembley finals. I first started going to Wembley with school. We'd go on the train at midnight and always went to see the ice hockey after the final. It was always the same two teams, Wembley Lions and Brighton Tigers. Then we went to London Palladium. They were great school trips. I saw Shirley Bassey there, Lonnie Donegan, The Platters and Johnny Ray as kids on the Wembley trips. I remember Hull getting to Wembley in 1959 and being thrashed by Wigan. I couldn't believe it. We had a dreadnought pack. We were invincible and what we weren't going to do to Wigan. And we got stuffed by a record score. All I remember is Tommy Finn getting Hull's only try and it was shown on telly at the

James Leuluai scores for Hull against Featherstone Rovers at Wembley in 1983.

The kick that broke Hull hearts. Featherstone's Steve Quinn kicks the late penalty goal that gave his side a 14-12 victory at Wembley in 1983.

beginning of 'Grandstand' week after week. So we could always say we scored more Wembley tries on TV than anybody else. But we were always the bridesmaid at Wembley. It was always, 'Oh no, here we go again.' Then you have to live with the taunts. I was only about fourteen when Hull first got to Wembley, so I couldn't drown my sorrows, although I might have sneaked a couple of pints. We used to go down with the supporters' club. The feeling after the

finals was bad, real bad. You'd see grown men crying. I did it once myself and that was when we got beat by Featherstone Rovers. I was with this hard case who used to play for Dockers Club and had a short fuse. There were these Featherstone fans laughing at me because I was crying like a baby. I was inconsolable. There I was, a grown man, a businessman who ran a factory with 108 people, crying my eyes out. And this hard case I was with said 'The next one who laughs at him is going to get flattened. Can't you see he's gutted?' Then we all went off and got drunk. Another thing was Rovers' fans throwing 10-5 in your face. You know, that was the score they beat us by at Wembley. I stood to win a lot of money on the Hull and Rovers final. Hull had played Millom amateurs in the first round and – I have a bit of a big gob on me – I said we'll easily beat these and we'll go on and win the Cup. Well, I'd had a few pints and I was worth a bob or two in them days and I said I'll have a grand on Hull to win the Cup. I couldn't back down, so I gave bookie Lennie Young the money and he backed it all the way through. He used to do what they called 'ring the bookie' in that area where they were playing and he'd say we'll get the extra point, what he called the tripe clippings. He said I'll get you the tripe clippings on this and he kept asking if I wanted to lay the bet off. By the time we'd finished and Hull played Rovers in the final I stood to win £18,500 because of the way we had invested. When we got to Wembley, he said 'Mick, you would never let me lay it off. Well, I've done so.' That meant I went down to Ross's on Hawthorne Avenue and picked up the princely sum of 3,200 quid.

Mike Adamson

Kevin James opens the scoring against Wigan in the 1985 Challenge Cup final.

Singing When We're Losing

Going to Wembley has been heartbreaking because we never won there. I remember when we'd lost yet again and all the fans were lining up at King's Cross Station ready for coming home. There were long lines snaking through the station. We were all pretty depressed. Suddenly one voice started singing 'Oooold Faithful…'. Then everybody took it up and it was beautiful. It just rang out in that great big old railway station. And that's when we lost. What would it be like if we ever won at Wembley?

Eric Gibbons

The Crying Game

Obviously, the Cup final at Wembley against Rovers sticks out. I don't remember going to see Hull at Wembley and not crying as a kid. My mum and dad ran a coach trip and took a load of friends to that game. We were all wearing really big rosettes and stupid hats. The match against Featherstone was awful because we thought we were really going to win at Wembley at last. I finished in floods of tears again. I seem to remember they took our half-back, Harkin, out early on. To lose to a last minute penalty after we'd got back into the game was heartbreaking. But even when we'd gone in front I didn't assume we were going to win. I'm the eternal pessimist. I'm never confident until the game is literally in the bag. Even when we were going down to the game and everybody thought winning was a formality I had my doubts. The 1985 final against Wigan was a real roller-coaster. We scored the first try, by Kevin James, then Wigan went well ahead and at 28-12 I think

it was you're ready to go. Then Hull started pegging it back. You're desperately looking at your watch, thinking are we going to nick this. But my usual pessimism said we'd no chance. I was absolutely gutted at the end. It was no consolation whatsoever that it was supposedly the greatest final ever. I couldn't care less about that. I'd have been a lot happier if we'd won 1-0. I was totally distraught. It's my biggest regret that they never won at the old Wembley and they never will now, although if they won the Cup at the new stadium I would class that as having won at Wembley. That's all we want. They've done everything else since I started watching them in 1979. When they took the final to Murrayfield I thought sod's law means Hull will win the Cup this year. And when they got to the semi-final I thought this is it. But they didn't get to the final. The only time we've won the Cup since they took it to Wembley was when we beat Widnes in the replay and that was at Elland Road. We got there real early and had a cracking view behind the goal at the end Hull were attacking in the second half and Crooks got his late try. But I saw virtually none of the first half at all because there were queues of people trying to get in, flooding into the lower tier and we were on the front row of the upper tier. So the bottom tier was absolutely packed and they couldn't get out. But there was a bit of room behind us, so there were people being dragged over our heads for the first twenty-five minutes. I was only twelve and my sister, who was two years younger, was there as well. She rarely went to games, but went to the big ones. I remember a policeman trying to climb over into the crowd and his helmet fell off onto her head. She burst into tears. So it was all a bit chaotic and I missed Toppo's great run-around moves that

Gary Divorty dives over for a try as Hull's fightback gathers momentum in the 1985 final against Wigan at Wembley.

brought tries, although I've seen it lots of times on the video since. But it was a great atmosphere and I remember falling asleep in the back of the car on the way home. That was my ultimate contentment, dropping off to sleep with Hull having won the Cup.

Ian Roberts

Divided School

I went to the Hull-Rovers final at Wembley with school. I lived in Hedon, which is sort of East Hull and obviously the vast majority on the bus were Rovers fans with about five of us Hull supporters. We had a great time going down, us five, giving them loads of stick. But you can imagine they got their own back after Rovers won. I was obviously upset at losing, although the magnitude of it doesn't hit you until years later. But the occasion was great for the city. One of the greatest matches for me has to be the Elland Road replay. We had good seats for that but we missed the first five minutes because our coach was held up in the traffic. Some people didn't get in until half-time. To win

Wembley jinx haunts Hull

Hull 24, Wigan 28

By RAYMOND FLETCHER

HULL are fated never to win at Wembley. That seems the only explanation after Saturday's remarkable Silk Cut Challenge Cup final in which they scored more points than any other beaten side at the stadium.

In fact only four winning teams had scored more. It was also the third time Hull have scored as many tries as the opposition and they are still without a win after six Wembley appearances.

Few winning teams have played better than Hull. They equalled Wigan's five tries in a scoring spectacular that was a glorious way to mark Wembley's 50th final. It was certainly the most entertaining of the 27 I have seen with the last 20 minutes packed with almost unbearable drama and suspense as Hull pulled back from 28-12 down.

To score five top quality tries without kicking the goals added to Hull's frustration and anguish. Although Crooks succeeded with his two penalty shots, he missed with three other kicks and Schofield was off target twice.

The match was a triumph for modern rugby played at a breath-taking pace with few stoppages. All but one of the ten tries — another Wembley record — were scored by backs as Wigan showed that wingers can still play an important and exciting role.

Ferguson's two superb tries and Gill's memorable 75-yard touchdown were proof of that as Wigan opened out in classic style. With Hull's James also touching down the four tries were the most totalled by wingers at Wembley.

And never have so many other players fulfilled Wembley's greatest expectations. Although Wigan's Kenny became the first Australian to win the Lance Todd Trophy two of his fellow countrymen Ferguson and Hull's Sterling, gave performances that would have won the man of the match award in many other years.

Kenny was all that Wigan hoped and Hull feared he would be. The Australian Test stand-off slipped out passes from the tightest of situations and glided effortlessly through openings.

It was Kenny who kept the ball alive after the fifth tackle for Potter's long pass to send Ferguson skipping round O'Hara for Wigan's first try in the 17th minute.

Then Kenny went away in majestic style for his try ten minutes later. He seemed to be only cantering when Ford put him away near halfway but his beautifully controlled running swept him past Kemble on a curving run to the corner.

Wigan's third try followed a long pass from Kenny that enabled Stephenson to launch Gill on a thrilling 75-yard dash up the touchline stepping out of despairing tackles by Sterling and Kemble for a great score just before half-time.

Kenny struck again just after the restart to twist round Sterling and give Edwards a clear 25-yard run

to the posts. He had already done enough to win the individual award but Sterling almost snatched it from him as he refused to accept defeat.

His immediate reply was to tear into the Wigan defence with a slashing 35-yard charge to within a yard of the line before hooking out a pass for Evans to score in the corner.

Sterling had also been involved in Hull's first try when he figured twice in the same move and his non-stop efforts enabled him to put Divorty over in the 74th minute.

There was also a top class performance from Norton. This was Hull's former Test loose forward proving he still has no superior when it comes to taking the ball in and creating play for others.

Hull could not have wished for a better performance from Leuluai, playing his first match after a three-week lay off with a shoulder injury. The New Zealand centre began Hull's three tries in a 12 minute blitz in the last quarter with a snappy try and finished it with a scorching 65-yard effort.

With just four minutes left Hull made a final run for glory and they almost achieved it at the last gasp as Evans battled to get clear from halfway but could not quite escape Wigan's desperate tackling.

A match worthy of the occasion

By BILL BRIDGE

WEMBLEY for once provided a match worthy of comparison to those long-gone black-and-white Eddie Waring days of Wigan and Hunslet, of Van Vollenhoven and Large.

The afternoon was perfect, the massive crowd in good humour — Wiganites seeming to outnumber their Hull FC opposites by at least two-to-one — and much of the rugby was of far and away better class than that seen (admittedly on the box) from the Twickenham Sevens.

Of course the scrums were a mess, they always are. But it still seems strange to hear League men talking of taking the ball "against the head." Next they will be believing that the kick at goal following a try is a conversion.

Hull's start was electric and deserved more than that well-worked try from James. When Wigan struck back Ferguson was superb but Hull's defence threadbare.

O'Hara and Kemble were exposed throughout the

game by Wigan's hard-running Ferguson. Kenny and Gill all scored tries which solid tackling would have prevented but nothing could have halted Leuluai's searing burst from his own half which turned the possibility of a revival from Hull into a week-long last five minutes for Wigan's suddenly subdued revellers.

Their response to Kenny's success in convincing the RL scribes of his claim to the Lance Todd Trophy was entirely predictable.

That magnificent Hull rally must have had those waverers for whom Wigan's success tipped the scales for Kenny on the edges of their seats, but for this refugee from Twickenham there were only two runners for the Lance Todd, neither Australian.

If it had to be a player then Norton was the man. His running, tackling and ball-handling skills were brilliant. But the man who really made the game what it became was the faultless referee Ron Campbell from Widnes.

Yorkshire Post *report of the 1985 final.*

Lee Crooks has Peter Sterling in support as he is well held in the 1985 final against Wigan.

was great because of the ribbing we'd had from Rovers fans. I don't remember much about coming back because I drunk that much and the coach was just awash with beer. We were hoping it would go slower just to make it all last longer. We weren't bothered about getting back.

Mike Poole

Pregnant Pause

The trips to Wembley were great and once we had to stop the bus because one of the women was pregnant and wanted a pee. So she went down an embankment and all the other women followed. Then a cop car came roaring up and said to us blokes 'If you can't take your beer don't sup it'. But one of us said 'It's my wife, she's pregnant.' And the copper said 'What? Every woman must be pregnant down your street.' Losing at Wembley was terrible, especially when we lost to Featherstone. We didn't think we could lose and as we were going into the ground, I said to this copper 'I tell you what pal, if Hull lose this game you can have our lass, my wife.' And she was alongside me. Of course, we got beat and the copper was there waiting when we came out. 'Is she still mine?' he asked. I had to say no. But we had some good times going to Wembley and every time Hull got to there I had to write a song about all the players. I sang it to James Leuluai and Gary Kemble when they came in the pub once. The worst Wembley has got to be losing 10-5 to Rovers. It still hurts now when you see they've got a web site 10-5.co.uk. Elland Road was my finest hour when we won the Cup in the replay. Widnes had walloped us in the Premiership a few days before, so beating them in the Cup final was unbelievable. I'll never forget that. The only thing to spoil it was when we got on the bus to go home the driver wouldn't stop it for a beer. We'd been singing and dancing after the match, so we might have got back to the bus a bit late. But we offered the driver a couple of quid apiece and there was about eighty of us on the bus and he still went right through without stopping. That put a right damper on the night.

Bob Cone

Wembley Baby

I was born on 30 April 1982 and my dad was at Wembley that weekend to see Hull play Widnes. So I think I was born on a special day. It's like people can remember where they were when Kennedy was shot. Well I know what I was doing when Hull got to Wembley in 1982. I was being born.

Craig Jessop

A Try to Forget

You'd think I'd remember some Hull tries from Wembley, but the ones that come to mind were scored by the opposition and you

thought 'Oh no'. The one I wish I couldn't remember was by Stuart Wright for Widnes in the 1982 final. He was one of those players who, because he was a winger, came in for quite a bit of stick from the Threepenny Stand lot. He had that long, Seventies permed hair, so that didn't help him. He was quite a good winger actually and I can remember a sunny Wembley. Hull were getting on top and attacking when there was this beautiful long pass out to the wing. I was thinking 'Yes, yes it's a try'. Then there was a strange sensation of seeing the ball floating out and wondering 'What's up?' And what's up is that bloody Stuart Wright has got the ball in his hands and is racing off for the line at the other end. My impression then is of 20,000 Hull fans with their heads in their hands. That was probably the worst moment I can think of. There is something cruel about interception tries anyway.

Trevor Gordon

Wembley Refugees Packed Station

Hull and Wembley. I've only get to think about it and I get depressed. I've seen all six of Hull's finals at Wembley and like thousands of others never seen them win there. My earliest recollections are of the aftermath of the 1959 final against Wigan. Hull were pretty well fancied to win but they got beat by a then record score. The thing I remember most is not the game but King's Cross Station round about midnight after the match. It was a like a wartime scene with bodies lying all over the place. Many of them had drowned their sorrows with a good booze up and were sleeping it off like so many refugees. We were there again the following

Hull's Kevin James (left) and Peter Sterling are close behind Wigan winger Henderson Gill as they all watch Shaun Edwards go down to collect the ball in the 1985 final at Wembley.

year and got another record hiding from Wakefield Trinity. But Hull were badly hit by injuries and half of their feared pack was missing. It was quite close at half-time and then Tommy Harris got concussed and Hull collapsed. So it was another pile up of bodies on the station. You had to feel sorry for them and it was the same every time they played at Wembley. Harris was the hero because he played on when injured and won the Lance Todd Trophy as man of the match. I remember going to see Hull come back from Wembley a day or two later and there was still quite a few to welcome them back on Paragon Station. The Featherstone final was

hardest to take. I mean Hull were winning 12-5, Featherstone were down to twelve men and there were only about fifteen minutes left. And we still lost. I heard a story about a Hull KR fan who walked out when Hull were winning because he couldn't stand the sight of them going up for the Cup. But he put the radio on and when Featherstone started coming back he returned to see Hull get beat. It looks as if Hull are fated never to win at Wembley. I mean, they scored as many tries as the opposition in their last four trips there and still never won. That's weird.

Charles Arnold

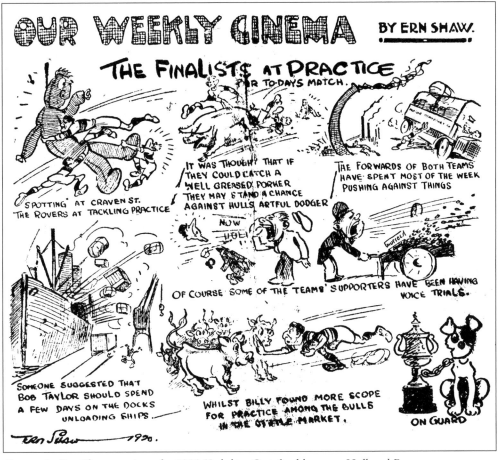

Cartoonist Ern Shaw previews the 1920 Yorkshire Cup final between Hull and Rovers.

Holiday Treat

The matches with Rovers were special to me as a youngster, partly because they were played at holiday times and that meant a trip up from Essex where we living then. So for about five years they were the only games I saw because we'd stay at grandma's for Christmas and one of the highlights used to be the Boxing Day derby with Rovers. I used to get really nervous about the matches. It was like if Hull beat Rovers twice a year that was the season sorted out. Whoever won, it meant a bad day at work for the losers. And as a kid I was always impressed by the big crowds. Yet I didn't go to see Hull at the Rovers ground that often. Even my dad didn't go. We were desperately mad keen Hull fans and even when Craven Park was only a couple of miles away we didn't go, simply because it was Rovers' ground. The gap was that big. It was more than just the river separating us. I started going to Craven Park when I got older and standing near that big greyhound tote board, thinking what a funny little ground it was. I remember writing about a Rovers player in the school magazine. I was at Beverley Grammar and bit of an oddity because I was a mad Hull FC fan. Anyway, the school had a magazine and every year some of the older boys interviewed a local celebrity. They did people like Philip Larkin the poet, Alan Plater the playwright and some Hull City soccer player. One year they decided to do Roger Millward, who was then captain of Rovers and England Rugby League. But they had no one in the school who knew anything about him or rugby league. So I went along for my first journalistic assignment. He was a Rovers player, of course, but we'll let that pass.

Trevor Gibbons

Coaches Roger Millward (Rovers) and Arthur Bunting (Hull) lead out their teams for a 1980 derby battle at Craven Park.

Family Differences

I miss the derby games against Rovers. There's no comparison with those games. There was 13,000 at The Boulevard when they were in the First Division a couple of years back. As much as I don't like Rovers, I think it's a shame the way they are now and I'd like them to be up there so we could play them. Believe it or not my wife is a Rovers supporter. All her family is from East Hull, while I'm from West Hull. We have our odd little thing about it, but it's not too bad. She doesn't go to Rovers now because I drag her down to Boulevard. She enjoys it because she likes to watch a good side. I take my sons

Hull and Hull Kingston Rovers fans come together for the 1980 Challenge Cup final at Wembley.

ONLY ROOM FOR ONE!

Opposing captains Jim Kennedy (Hull) and Arthur Moore (Rovers) play musical chairs before the 1920 Yorkshire Cup final.

now and they're solid Hull fans. Especially the little one. One's two and a half and he's got the shirt. The other one's five and he was a Rovers supporter to start with, but I've got him round to Hull.

David Boast

Only One Team in Hull

I've always been upset that when you go out of the traditional rugby league areas and you mention Hull they always reply with Hull Kingston Rovers. But as far as I'm concerned there's only one team in Hull. It was great

when the two clubs were great sides, but only as long as we were winning.

Simon Shaw

Something Special

I miss the Hull and Rovers games. They were something special. They wouldn't be the same now because they wouldn't be competitive. I hated Rovers and still do, but I'd love to see them in the Super League competing with us again, just so we could beat them. There were no better times than when Hull and Rovers were the two best teams around. The matches between them were great. The atmosphere was incredible. I remember going to Rovers and we were winning 18-0 and still got beat. In them days to get beat from 18-0 was unheard of. Now I still look for Rovers' result and hope they've got beat. It makes your week if Hull have won and Rovers have lost.

Andy Scarah

Granddad was a Rovers Fan

I want Rovers to have a decent team because there is a big rivalry with them. My granddad was a Rovers fan through and through and there was always a lot of rivalry between him and my dad. I used to like it when Hull played Rovers, especially at The Boulevard. What an atmosphere there was then. The stands would be packed. Even though the clubs don't meet each other now, there is still that rivalry. You only have to listen to the local radio five o'clock phone-ins on Sundays to hear the fans having a go at each other.

Mally Foston

Generated Interest

I miss the old derby games against Rovers. They generated a lot of interest. It was the hatred of each other. I don't mean in a nasty way, although there was some nastiness. I like to hate them. I don't go as far as not eating bacon because it's red and white, but when they lose we do a bit of cheering. I'd like to play Rovers again, so we could beat them, but I wouldn't want them in Super League. It's maybe being nasty, but I don't really want them to progress.

Peter Oglesby

Early Teachings

I saw a few of the derby matches against Rovers and they were really good. I was taught from an early age not to like Rovers. It wasn't allowed. But it came easy, anyway. I think I'd like us to be playing them again and beating them by a large margin, but then I think it's good that they are in the Northern Ford Premiership because it means we're better than them. I've seen photographs of when they played each other at Christmas and it must have been great then with really big crowds.

Matt Smith

Plateful of Fun

In 1997 we played Rovers at Craven Park after they had won the Silk Cut Plate at Wembley. There were more Hull fans than Rovers fans and we all took along paper plates to wind Rovers up about winning the Mickey Mouse trophy they had just won. We like to do that sort of thing.

Ben Horsley

Hull's Johnny Whiteley dives over for a try from a scrum in an RL Challenge Cup-tie against Rovers in 1959.

RUGBY LEAGUE

in

CORNWALL

HULL

v.

HULL KINGSTON ROVERS

MONDAY, 4th JUNE at PENZANCE kick-off 7-15
TUESDAY, 5th JUNE at CAMBORNE kick-off 7-15

Hull and Rovers made a three-match exhibition tour of Cornwall in 1962.

Real Battles

The matches with Rovers were always battles. They really got stuck into each other. I remember when they met in the late Seventies in the Challenge Cup first round at The Boulevard. Rovers had two players sent off, Phil Lowe and Colin Tyrer I think, and Hull's Alf Macklin scored the winner in the corner. He wasn't the fastest winger but he had a big overlap because Rovers were two players short.

John Atkinson

Horrendous

There was an animosity between the fans but it never turned into anything very nasty apart from that Good Friday when the bricks flew. It was horrendous at the time, but generally it was always in good humour. For some reason the Hull fans always seemed to pick on George Fairbairn, the Rovers full-back. We used to sing 'Georgie Girl' at him.

Tony Green

Caught Out in Red and White

I hated Rovers, absolutely hated them. When they won the Cup, the first match back at Craven Park was sponsored by a friend of mine, another businessman. He knew nothing about rugby league and he asked to me go and judge the Man of the Match. I had to go in that bar at Rovers and as I walked through the door, Percy Johnson and Bill Land, Rovers directors, stuck the Challenge Cup in my hand with red and white rosettes. They also put a red and white hat on my head and took a photograph of me. They showed everybody this photo with me as a turncoat. So when we went across to Australia I got one of Rovers' dyed-in-the-wool supporters in a black and white shirt and videoed him. Percy called all his Hull FC friends black and white bastards. The worst period was when Rovers started getting on top. They had forwards like Frank Foster and we had Eric Broom at prop. I'm told Frank used to ring him up before a derby game and scare him to death.

Mike Adamson

The Greatest Rivalry

As much as I love Rovers losing, I wish we were still playing them. They were the

Referee Ron Campbell gets caught up in a 1984 derby brawl.

matches you always looked forward to all year. We always said it didn't matter how many matches you lost, as long as you beat Rovers twice. It seems strange now but before I started going to matches I'd support either Hull or Rovers, whoever won the last match because my best mate was a Rovers fan. But my mum called me to one side one day and said 'This pretending to be a Rovers fan has got to stop because you're upsetting your dad.' It annoys me when you hear commentators saying there's no bigger game or rivalry in rugby league than Wigan and St Helens or Leeds and Bradford. They can't have been to a Hull and Rovers match. One of the best was the Floodlit

Trophy final when Hull beat them at The Boulevard. It was one of the first games I went to. My dad took me and my mate from school. We got there late for some reason and we couldn't get anywhere near Threepenny Stand. We ended up at the scoreboard end and couldn't see a thing. So my dad ripped up a bit of this fence that ran round the back and we stood on the crossbar of the fence to watch the game. I do remember that the only time I wanted Rovers to win a game they let me down. That was when we were in the running for the championship and played Widnes at the end of the season. We absolutely tonked them, but we needed Rovers to win at Leigh to stop them winning the title. It was a really sunny day and when our match finished, a lot of the crowd went on the pitch and listened to the Leigh and Rovers match on Radio Humberside which they put over the Tannoy. Rovers lost, so Leigh took the championship. I was never in favour of the moves to merge with Rovers. In fact, I was once on a course for work to do with presentation skills. You had to put together a five or ten minute presentation to put to the rest of the people on the course and mine was on why a merger between Hull and Rovers wouldn't work. I felt a city the size of Hull can support two clubs. Now we don't play Rovers, it seems Leeds have taken their place for us to hate. I think you need that. Not in a nasty way, but it's part of watching your team.

Ian Roberts

We Want Rovers Back

I think if we could get Hull and Rovers back in one division it would be great because it generates interest. When they were both in the First Division they were always talking about rugby in the pubs, the banter and rivalry was great. I still know kids who are Rovers supporters but it's just not the same with us not playing each other. I didn't hate Rovers, that's too strong a word, but we really did want to beat them. In fact, they do a lot of fund-raising for Rovers where I still live in Hedon and I always contribute to that. Most Hull supporters love to get the better of Rovers, but if they're honest they want them in the same division. We want them there to beat them.

Mike Poole

Always Somebody Sent Off

The derby games with Rovers were really hard games, and the crowd egged them on. There was always somebody sent off. You might get the odd dirty player now, but then they took everybody's head off. Half-arming was part of the game and they were always carrying players off. The plan was to stick the scrum-half away. Hull had a scrum-half called Teddy Mills, who was five foot tall and weighed seven stones, like a jockey. But he would tackle big forwards round the bootlaces and bring them down. I remember Hull and Rovers played one night and it poured down. I got soaked to the skin and after the game I got back to the car and I couldn't operate the pedals because my trousers were so wet. So I slipped them off and drove home. When I got back I was stood ringing the bell with my trousers over my arm. My wife was upstairs bathing the kids, but young Jeremy had come down and was shouting up to her: 'Mam, there's dad outside with no trousers on'. What she thought I'd been up to after telling her I'd gone to see Hull and Rovers I don't know.

Aubrey Coupland

Craven Park Highlights

I don't hate Rovers, but my mate's a Rovers fan and I bought him a video of Craven Park highlights and all that was on it was greyhound racing and speedway. Some used to have a whip-round and buy a Rovers shirt before a derby game and then set fire to it in Threepenny Stand. There was no danger of the stand getting on fire

Hull loose forward Steve Norton pops his head above a scrum to keep an eye on Rovers scrum-half Roger Millward during a 1978 RL Challenge Cup-tie. Keith Hepworth also keeps watch.

because it was always sopping wet through and you know what with.

Bob Cone

Friends Apart

I used to love the derby games and beating Hull KR, but I wouldn't say I hated the Robins. In fact, my best friend was a Rovers fan. We were born down the same terrace and he became as red and white as you could be and I became as black and white as you could be. His middle name is Robin and his late father had been one of the first ever passholders at Hull KR.

Steve Roberts

Hull Strike After Beating Rovers

The earliest Hull and Rovers match I can remember was about fifty years ago when a reserve team winger called Sanders was brought in on the wing for somebody who was injured. He scored all three tries in Hull's win and went right back into the A team. In fact, I don't think he played many first games at all. That could also have been the match that caused Hull's players to go on strike. They wanted extra money for beating Rovers and when they didn't get it I think the players went on strike and missed a couple of games. Rovers weren't a good team but Hull's players obviously thought meeting them was still one of the hardest games of the

Jim Macklin turns the ball inside to Clive Sullivan during the 1969 match against Hull Kingston Rovers.

season. I used to love the derby games at The Boulevard. You'd get 25,000 packed into The Boulevard and they would bring in ringside seats, a very appropriate name, round the field. Rovers fans had to take some ribbing from the Threepenny Stand as they walked the full length of the pitch to get to their seats. I remember them playing at Boothferry Park a few times. They were Rovers' home matches and Hull City, who were quite well off then, loaned them the ground. The match that sticks out is a floodlit game when Harry Markham made some powerful runs down the right hand touch. What a forward.

The atmosphere was terrific. Fans hated each other, but not in a nasty way. I remember it mostly as good humoured. Mind you I've known it break up relations. When Hull and Rovers played at Wembley there was one young couple who supported different teams and they made a pact that whoever won they'd stay to cheer them. But when Rovers won the Hull fan walked off. 'I'm not cheering for them,' she said, left her boyfriend and never met him again.

Charles Arnold

CHAPTER 6

Black and White Forever

A packed Threepenny Stand watches Hull take on Bradford Northern in 1984.

RUGBY LEAGUE REVIEW

The Journal of Rugby League Football
FIFTH YEAR CONTINUOUS PUBLICATION   EDITOR—STANLEY CHADWICK

| Vol. 5 No. 108 | FRIDAY, NOVEMBER 17th, 1950 | Price 7d. |

HULL
R.L. OUTPOST—BUT NOT OUTCASTS!

Left to Right.
Back Row (Standing)—C. O'Leary, J. Clark, T. Hart, D. Foreman, D. Rushton, S. Harrison, T. Danter, A. Bedford.
Front Row (Seated)—M. Scott, E. Lawrence, R. L. Francis (Capt.), K. Gittoes, T. Harris.
In Front (Kneeling)—I. Watts, D. Burnell.

Photograph by "Rugby League Review" Cameraman R. A. Clayborn.

Rugby League Review *cover sums up Hull's status in 1950.*

Old Faithful to the End

I'm a Hull fan myself, but I'd rather talk about my father-in-law, Charlie Rowlin, who was a really big supporter and hit the headlines when he died, because I propped him up on the bus to bring him back home from the Cup final at Murrayfield. He was seventy-seven and had been very ill for sometime, but nothing was going to stop him going to his fifty-first Cup final. It was a regular trip, even if Hull weren't playing. He'd enjoyed the final, had a few drinks and we went back to the hotel. I shared a room with him and when he didn't wake up in the morning I knew the worst had happened. I just wanted to take him home without causing any fuss. So I dressed him in his best suit, pulled his black and white Hull FC cap slightly over his eyes and a mate helped me to carry him onto the bus. We propped him up in his seat and didn't tell anyone else until we were well on the way home. There was a brief silence and then everybody, all his old mates, started singing *Old Faithful.* It was great. He would have loved that. They also sang it at the funeral service, including the vicar and he said not to tell anybody because he was a Rovers fan. The cortege had gone past The Boulevard so Charlie could say a last farewell to the ground. He was a regular at The Yorkshireman pub, where I'm the landlord, and there's a plaque that says *Charlie's Corner.* It's above a painting of the Threepenny Stand, which has a frame made of wood from the old stand.

John O'Loughlin

Boulevard Means Everything to Me

They all used to come into the supporters' club in the old days. They weren't separate like they are now. It had been open forty-seven years when it closed down. We helped to build it, my husband and I. They used to have all the presentations in the club. The players were the same as us, if you get what I mean. They all had to have jobs. It's different now in Super League. I still go to the matches, but I think some of the friendliness is missing. It used to be a lovely atmosphere. The Boulevard means everything to me. My children, a boy and a girl, were brought up on rugby and are both shareholders. My grandchildren were also brought up on rugby. They used to say Ivy and Ernie are out there in all kinds of weather. Years ago, when they didn't have a supporters' club, they used to have meetings under the stand and we'd take them cocoa.

Ivy Mason

Three Hours to Halifax

When they re-formed the Hull Supporters' Club after the war, I was one of the founder members and we eventually built a clubhouse. We had a pretty good relationship with the directors at that time, such as Ernie Hardaker. A good man he was. We used to run buses to every away match. We'd leave from outside the Regal cinema. I remember once we took five coaches to Halifax. One year the driver didn't know the way to the Thrum Hall ground, but on the edge of Halifax we saw these local supporters and they got on the bus to guide us to the ground. Then after the match a Halifax supporter took a bus-load of us for a meal and a drink. That was before the motorways and it would take us about three hours. I can remember perhaps only a couple of times going by train. Our furthest trips would be to Workington and Whitehaven and

General views of The Boulevard during a Humberside XIII v. All Stars benefit match for Tommy Harris and Brian Cooper in 1960. Above: Looking towards the Airlie Street end as Wigan's All Star Billy Boston scores. Below: Bunker's Hill at the Gordon Street end is the back drop as Wigan's Mick Sullivan heads for the line. The volunteer touch judge is former Hull winger Ivor Watts.

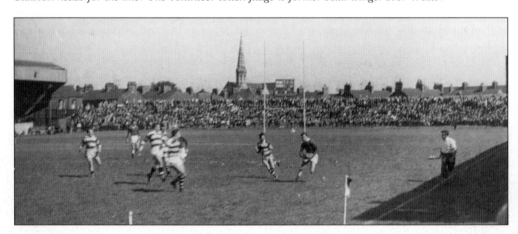

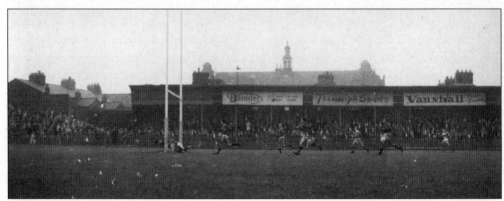

Above: The old Chiltern Street School overlooks the Threepenny Stand in 1960. Both of these once familiar sights have long since been demolished, apart from a small section of the stand on the left of the photograph.

we'd have set off at about seven in the morning. Unlike recent years, we were always welcomed on away grounds. I don't recall in over forty years ever seeing any real violence. There were arguments, but the humour was very witty. We used to insult each other tremendously, but there was no fisticuffs that I saw. If we went to Leeds after the match we would go to Burley Liberal Club and have a good night mingling with the Leeds people.

Ernie Mason

It's Hull or Nothing

I've lived in Baildon for the past fifteen years. But I'm from Hull originally and if the worst came to the worst, and at one time it looked as if Hull would go out of existence, I couldn't have followed another team. To be honest, I would probably have stopped going to rugby a lot. The nearest team to me is the Bradford Bulls and I don't think I would go there. I don't drive but I go to as many Hull matches as I can. Rugby kits in general are not what they were. I wouldn't buy one now because they don't seem like proper shirts. If you're paying £40 I think you want more than a bit of polyester, which probably cost two or three quid to make. But I'm glad Hull have gone back to something like their traditional strip. Everybody changes their colours now but when I started to watch Hull in 1965 they'd

Hull and Hunslet teams line up before the Spring Bank Orphanage Challenge Cup charity match in 1912/13. The legendary Billy Batten is in the white-shirted Hunslet team on the back row next to the Cup, but by the end of the season he had joined Hull in a record-breaking transfer.

been playing in those colours for most of the century without alteration.

Keith Jenkinson

It's in My Blood

I still wear the old irregular black and white hoops shirt. I've got the others, but this is the one that means most to me. I didn't like it when they were Hull Sharks, but dropping the Airlie Birds didn't bother me. It's the three crowns that counts and *Old Faithful,* of course. I can sing all the words to that. Hull means a lot to me. I could have watched football at Hull City, but it's a rugby town. When Hull were doing badly last season I was still there, because it's in my blood. It's like a religion. I was brought up in Threepenny Stand. It's part of my bringing up, what happened in there. The atmosphere, the humour. It was fantastic. There was swearing, but it was good-humoured. Nowt really bad. You could have a laugh even with the opposing players.

Stephen Buckley

I Like Tradition

I'd prefer that the club stayed at The Boulevard, but I know things probably have to change. Like I was glad that we merged with Gateshead because it meant we'd survived. But I think they will have to generate a lot more support if they do move to a new ground, because they'll lose a lot of the atmosphere in a bigger stadium. I prefer the traditional things like the black and white jersey. And I must admit I prefer winter rugby. I used to love getting wrapped

up. I would rather have my gloves and my woolly scarf on.

Kim Brindley

Characters Still There

Hull FC is a big part of my life without a shadow of a doubt. We start building up for the match on a Thursday. And if the match is on Sky on the Friday, we start talking about it on the Tuesday. When the *Hull Daily Mail* arrives I'm fighting over it with my wife to read what the team is and which players have picked up a knock. We first started going to matches together before we were married. I think she went out of sufferance then, but she's real keen now and will go on her own when I can't get there. I'd miss The Boulevard if we had to move to another ground. The new grounds, like the McAlpine Stadium, are hollow. There's no atmosphere. But The Boulevard has a special atmosphere. Although the old wooden Threepenny Stand has gone, the characters are still there. It won't be the same if they move.

Ian Anderson

Panicking

Following Hull can be depressing. Like when it looked as if we were going to get relegated. But I remember the last match that season. It was a must-win game and when we won it was like winning the Cup. Then it looked as if the club might have to pack up. We were panicking then. I couldn't imagine life without watching Hull on a Sunday. I would probably have started going

Hull team in 1909/10. Players only, from left to right, back row (standing): Holder, Walter, Herridge, Havelock. Middle row (seated): Devereux, Rogers, Taylor, Anderson, Connell, Morton, Boylen. Front row: Rogers, Wallace.

to watch Hull Kingston Rovers. It wouldn't have been the same as cheering for Hull FC, but I like my rugby too much now to give it up.

Carol Anderson

It's a Rugby Town

Hull FC is a big thing in my life now. Where I live, on Longhill Estate, everybody talks about rugby. It's a rugby town. I won a Hull strip for designing a new strip in the *Hull Daily Mail*. I just wanted the old irregular black and white hoops back. That's Hull. My brother's got all the old-fashioned shirts with V-neck collars and the present one is more or less like those. It's got to be black and white. I didn't like it when they had all other colours, especially that purple. That was awful. It would

bother me if we had to leave The Boulevard. I've grown up going there all the time and it won't be the same if and when we go to a new stadium. It's become a ritual going to The Boulevard. This is only the second season we've been going in Threepenny Stand. We used to go in the East Stand before. But there's more atmosphere in Threepenny Stand. They're a good-humoured crowd, but there's also a lot of swearing. It wasn't half as bad when I went as a kid to what it is now. But that's everyday banter now. We were at the semi-final at Huddersfield when some Hull fans invaded the pitch after the match was over and we thought that was disgusting. I signed the good behaviour charter after that and it was a good day when we went to the meeting, talking to the coach and officials about how we can make the club better.

Mally Foston

Les Barlow, a forward stalwart of Hull's 1936 Championship-winning team.

Hull Fans are Different

It would be a bit of a wrench to leave The Boulevard, but from what I've heard West Hull would still be playing there, so I don't think they'll ever close it down and we could make a pilgrimage to it. Atmosphere has a lot to do with it all. I remember going to every match home and away for two seasons with somebody I used to go to college with. It was just the atmosphere of going, meeting the same people and the banter. I remember going to Wigan once and we won something like 18-12 on a Wednesday night. We didn't get back until two the next morning. You tried to make the wins last as long as possible,

especially after winning at Wigan. But even when we got hammered we always had a good time. We once went to St Helens and we were getting stuffed. We had police all round us, the Hull fans. It was because they didn't know what to make of us. All we were doing was singing, even though we were beaten. They must have thought we were going to cause trouble, but we just walked out the ground singing and on to the coaches. The police looked baffled. No other club has fans like that. We're just different.

Paul Ashton-Worsnop

Some of the Atmosphere has Gone

Following Hull is really a big part of my life and I look forward to going every week. At the moment I'm quite lucky because my daughter works for a company that has an executive box, which I can go in. I've also got a season pass, so what I do is I give that day's ticket to somebody wearing a black and white shirt. Normally, I go in Threepenny Stand and always have done. It's not as good as when it was the old stand. It's lost a lot of its atmosphere since the problem at the McAlpine Stadium when some Hull fans got out of hand. It's quietened down too much. They had to stop the swearing, but I think they've taken too much of the atmosphere away with it.

Dave Worsnop

Shirt Spotting

The black and white shirt means a lot to me. I remember reading in *Open Rugby* magazine once that you could always spot a Hull fan a mile off if he was wearing the black and white irregular hoops. It's true. As soon as you see it you point and start talking about Hull no matter where you are in the world. Hull FC is a massive part of my life and I don't see what else could take its place.

Craig Jessop

Good Riddance to Sharks

The black and white hoops mean a lot to me. I wasn't happy when they moved away from it with Hull Sharks. There was no need for it. But I still went out and bought the shirt because it was Hull. I was glad when they came back to Hull FC even though it took a merger to do it. It saved the club and that was the main thing. To be honest, it couldn't have finished a great deal better for us because of the players we got. I would have liked to have seen them get out of trouble without having to merge with another club, but the situation didn't allow it. Leaving The Boulevard for another ground would be hard because there are a lot of memories there. But I would accept it reluctantly because it's progress.

Rob Dale

Turned Out for the Best

Following Hull is now a big part of my life. It takes up every weekend in the summer. A bad defeat will bother me for a couple of days before I can shrug it off. The Boulevard also means a lot to me because it creates such a great atmosphere, but you have to move on and the way forward is a super stadium. I think the crowd invasion at Huddersfield has had the effect of improving the club. You still get some idiots in Threepenny Stand chanting not appropriate songs, but you now get people telling them to be quiet. It has taken some of the fun away because some of the chants were really funny, but as a club we've got to clear the riff-raff out. Living away from Hull, I got a lot of hassle after the McAlpine trouble because I work in Leeds and I was quite embarrassed. That was an all-time low to be a Hull supporter. Generally though there is a lot of good banter with me being a Hull fan among Leeds and Bradford supporters. I get a few strange looks when I walk out in my Hull shirt and I quite like it. I also wear it away on holidays because I like to show it around.

Mike Beckett

Match day Ritual

I think of watching Hull as a relief valve at the end of the week. It's the one thing that I do. I go to relax and enjoy it. I love the game. I go to support the team. I remember, when we were always getting hammered, we were all stood there in Threepennies and we said 'Right, we're going home now. We've had enough.' And my daughter said 'I'll see you in the car then because I'm staying to support my team'. She was twelve and I thought if that's how she feels, it's doing her some good. It's putting something into her life. As much as I love Hull FC and The Boulevard, I'm not into this idea of we must stay at the ground. I've stood in Threepenny Stand all my life and it would be hard to leave that, but I think the club has got to move on. It is something that has got to happen at sometime or other. We can't stay in the past. And changing the shirts' colours never really bothered me. I'm not into the traditional thing. As long as it brings the club on and brings other people through the

FOOTBALL EXCURSION
MANCHESTER 13/6
(SWINTON v. HULL)
Saturday, 13th March
HULL ... ... 9- 2 a.m.
Arrive ... ... 11-38 a.m.
Return ... ... 5-53 p.m.
Due back Leeds ... ... 7-11 p.m.
Going forward from there
at 8-55 or 10-40 p.m.
Full details from the station
and usual agencies
BRITISH RAILWAYS

efore and after the match . . . . .
Call at
BEN'S
tadium Newsagency,
Airlie Street
for all your requirements in Tobacco,
Cigarettes, Sweets, Chocolate,
Ices, Magazines, etc.
ll Sports Magazines on sale !

Are You MOVING ?
ACROSS THE STREET . . . .
. . . ACROSS THE WORLD
HARDAKER'S
REMOVALS - STORAGE
BOULEVARD - HULL
Tel. 37493 - 37835

SOUTHAMS (HULL) LTD.
WINE AND SPIRIT MERCHANTS AND BEER BOTTLERS
WHOLESALE AND RETAIL
DELIVERIES MADE IN HULL AND EAST RIDING
Branches :
Agents in Hull and East Riding for :
Hull Brewery Ales, Bass & Guinness
804 Beverley High Road Tel. 8449
Watney's Ales and Stouts
270 Bricknell Avenue Tel. 8357
Hammerton Oatmeal Stout
419 Hessle Road Tel. 37091
Distributing Agents in Hull and District for
Main Street, Willerby Tel. 46058
Schweppes Minerals
109 ANLABY ROAD :: HULL
Telephone 16684

MARTIN RIBY'S, 47 ANLABY ROAD (Corner Midland Street)

5 HULL   Colours : Black and White   ATT. 20,000   REC. £1,912

Hutton 1G.

Bowman 2 / Riches 3 / Turner 4 / Watts 5

Conway 1T. 6 / Tripp 7

Scott 8 / Harris 9 / Coverdale 10 / Hockley 11 / Markham 12 / Whiteley 13

Referee : Mr. G. S. PHILLIPS (Widnes)   H.T. 2-5   Touch-Judges : Mr. A. CADY and Mr. W. JONES

Henderson 8 / Lymer 9 / Key 10 / Mudge 11 / Thompson 12 / Ivison 13

Archer 6 / Dawson 1T. 7

Ivill 5 / Gibson 4 / Paskins 3 / Southward 2

Risman 1G. 1

5 WORKINGTON TOWN   Colours : White with Blue Band

Any changes in the above sides will be announced immediately before the match

UNDERWEAR—WORKSHIRTS—BOOTS

OILSKINS—RUBBER BOOTS—Tel. No. 33006

SPECIALISTS IN INDUSTRIAL OVERALLS

FRED LORD   Telephone 38969
. . . Pays Cash for Scrap
BRASS, COPPER, LEAD, Etc. — RAGS, WOOL, ROPE
8 ETON STREET - HESSLE ROAD - HULL

FROSTWAYS LTD.
Telephone 52936
PRIVATE HIRE COACHES & TAXIS
RADIO LUXURY TRAVEL —— 21 ST. GEORGE'S ROAD, HULL

HULL DAILY MAIL
THE
GREEN SPORTS MAIL
For ALL REPORTS & RESULTS
EVERY SATURDAY

SUPPORTERS' CLUB NOTES

Last week I said we were in for a rea treat when Workington play here, an to-day I hope my wishes will be realise We are all looking forward to a capacit crowd and I would like to appeal to th good-nature of all to co-operate in packin so that all who wish to see the game ma do so in comfort.

We should see a thrilling match — an one that need not bear that time-wor tag of being just "typical Cup-tie foot ball" — both sides are good enough t give us something extra-special !

And will the sequence be kept up ? . . Widnes, Workington, Wembley ?

Join us to-day — Annual "Sub." onl 2/-.

Lucky Programme

Our Supporters' Club members will b selling the club programme to-day an there will be, on this occasion, THREE lucky numbers — the holders being each entitled to two free Stand tickets for ou next home League game.

"Regulars" on the West Stand have mentioned that they would prefer their usual position when they are the lucky winners — this can be done with pleasure and two free admission tickets for the West Stand can be had instead of the usual New Stand seats, if preferred.

Last week's winner was — Mr. G. W Higgins, 9, Beatrice Avenue, Linnaeus Street, from the West Side of the ground

Listen for the announcements at half-time, and claim your prizes either after the game to-day or by post.

COMING ATTRACTIONS

Next Saturday, March 13th, at 3 p.m. : Bradford Northern " A "

Saturday, March 20th, at 3 p.m. : Hull Kingston Rovers " A "

Centre pages of the programme for the Hull v. Workington Town RL Challenge Cup-tie in 1954.

gates, I don't mind. I didn't mind calling them The Sharks. It took a bit of getting used to, but after a season we were into it and my kids never knew anything different.

Andy Scarah

Proud to be Black and White

I was really sad when it looked as if we might not have an A-team last year. My little boy was as well, because he didn't think he would have an A-team to support. I was so pleased when Gateshead and Hull combined so that we still had an A-team. It meant we were still black and white and kept our name. It was important that we kept the black and white shirts. That's what they wore when I was a little girl. It made me proud. You get a lot of banter from the crowds, saying 'Get back to Gateshead', but it doesn't bother and I think it has been for the good of the club. Moving to a new stadium wouldn't bother me. I think it would be good for the town. But I probably haven't been going that long to have the sadness that an awful lot of people will have if we move to a new ground.

Christine Young

Family Hobby

It's a big hobby for us. My son and grandchildren go as well. My daughter used to go, my sister's kids used to go. It was a family outing. We all felt dreadful when it looked as if Hull might have to pack up. We'd gone to the last match and they really played their hearts out. David Lloyd had promised them £1,000 each if they won the match and when he turned round and said he was shutting the club down I think everybody could have killed him. It's a lot better now they play in summer. I used to be freezing and I'd stand and think 'Why am I here, freezing to death?' But when they scored we'd jump up and down and not feel the cold.

Doreen Scarah

Through Good and Bad Times

I was a Threepenny-stander and used to sit in there and watch Hull when they were rubbish. You could sit down because there was not that many went. I've been standing in there when you could hardly move it was that jam-packed. I've been through all the good and bad times. I've often said: 'That's it, I'm not going again', but I always do. If I can't get to a match I don't listen to them on radio. It just gets me. I'll tell the wife to turn it on for the score and, even if they're winning, I tell her to turn it off again. It would hurt a lot if Hull had to leave The Boulevard. But I think you have to move with the times and I'd still go. I know a lot of people have said they wouldn't, but I think after a couple of months they would. Even when we get thrashed, we're still there at the end singing and shouting. We never walk out early. Well, sometimes at

Castleford we do because of the traffic. But losing does hurt. I get a really bad feeling in my stomach. It's hard to explain, I just feel awful. I don't go around moping, but I feel a bit ill.

Barry Scarah

Put Under Stress

What does Hull FC mean to me? Put it this way, I was under a lot of stress when they were on about the merger and whether Hull FC were going to exist or not. I live in Grimsby and all my mates across in Hull were hearing bits and bobs and I was hearing nothing. It was pure Hell hearing nothing and not knowing what was going on. All I knew about it was bits in the paper and on Ceefax. When I heard they'd merged with Gateshead, it was a complete and utter surprise. As things turned out I was reasonably happy. Going back to the old black and white shirts won me over a bit. I'm sitting on the fence about leaving The Boulevard for a new stadium. There is reason to move, but there's also scope to redevelop the ground. I wouldn't want an all-seater because I prefer to stand. When you sit down you seem to be a bit away from it all. I always stand on Bunker Hill, near the scoreboard at the Airlie Street end. I've always called it Bunker Hill. I don't know why. I probably learnt it off my dad.

Graham Foot

Traditional Shirt Important

The black and white strip is important. The strip they played in when they were the Sharks was diabolical. Ask anybody in the

Hull take on the 1980 New Zealand tourists at Hull City's Boothferry Park. Keith Tindall is the man in possession.

crowd and 99.9 per cent would have told you they wanted them to play in black and white hoops. Tradition is very much a part of rugby league and I think sometimes the top brass don't recognise that. They try to make everything flash and modern to appeal to the younger kids. Same with the ground. I think the majority would sooner stay at The Boulevard. You would lose the atmosphere if you moved. I sit in the seats now in the new Threepenny Stand, but I preferred standing in the old one. We lost a lot of atmosphere when they put seats in. They should have rebuilt it as a concrete stand to stand in. The old stand holds a lot of memories for me. I learned a few new words in there. The stand used to be completely full in them days. Teams used to come to Boulevard and I'm sure half of them were frightened to death when they came out because of Threepenny Stand. I was part

of that and was happy to give the opposition a bit of stick. They used to say we were worth a five point start. It's not the same now. It's different when you're sat down. Hull FC is a big part of my life. When I go abroad on holiday I always get an English paper to see how Hull have got on. And they keep all the *Hull Daily Mails* for me to read when I get back. So I don't miss much.

John Atkinson

Hull Pride

Whatever people are like, you all become just a part of Hull when you go away. It's where you're from. You're proud to be from Hull and like to sing 'We are Hull'. I work in Leeds at the moment and when we played at Headingley I went all the way back to Hull to pick my friend, Mally, up in the car. I just love the game that much. I'd go anywhere to see Hull. I wish Paris still had A-team because I would have liked to have seen Hull play there. The atmosphere in Threepenny Stand has gone down since what happened at Huddersfield and I don't think I'll buy a pass for there next year. People swear at any match, it's not just the Hull fans. We always had good banter without causing any trouble. In all the years I've been going I can remember only a bit of an incident between a couple of fans. And I'd also like to go back to winter rugby because I don't mind standing in the cold. You can always get wrapped up. I think the atmosphere was better in winter as well. It was a muddy game and the players seemed to have more meat on them. That's how I liked it.

Mark Donoghue

Supreme Moment

When David Lloyd took over, we had come to the conclusion that it was all over. Kapput! I'll never forget coming back from work on the day the merger was announced. Ironically, I was on Marfleet Lane, near Rovers' ground and it was on the radio that we'd merged and were going to get Super League football. It couldn't have come at a more appropriate place – outside Rovers' ground because they were lauding the fact that we were dead and buried. It was a supreme moment.

Eric Gibbons

A Century of Support

I used to listen to my dad and Uncle Billy. All they talked about was the great Hull

team of the Fifties and especially their battles with Halifax. So I grew up thinking the likes of Tommy Harris, Mick Scott, Tommy Finn, Johnny Whiteley and the Drake twins had actually finished only about a year earlier because I knew so much about them. They were talked about as if they were superhuman. Sometimes the backs came into it, but it was nearly always about that pack. So when I became a real Hull fan I always felt I was carrying something on. My granddad, who was born in 1892, actually went to The Boulevard before the turn of the last century as a young lad. So at the end of the nineteenth century and through the whole of the last century into this one, you can trace a family line of Hull supporters from my granddad, through

1968 programme.

Hull's 1959 team that reached Wembley for the first time. From left to right, back row: Keegan, J. Drake, Sykes, W. Drake, Cooper, Scott. Middle row: Saville, Harris, Whiteley, Cowan, Watts. Front row: Matthews, Finn.

my dad and mum and now myself. It sometimes annoys me now that people talk about Super League as if nothing existed before then. I'm more of a rugby league fan generally now and don't go just to see Hull FC all that often. But there is still that bond and I realised it when there was that terrible time when David Lloyd was in a charge of the club. It was also bound up with that

dreadful season in Super League when they were down at the bottom. I realised then that I was still a great Hull fan because I went more and was concerned to see them when they were at the bottom than I would have done if they'd been at the top. I felt that I had to go. It was important to me. I saw some really bad games, like when they lost to Huddersfield. They were atrocious, but I stood in the standing Threepenny Stand and roared them on. The point is that I wanted to be there. It was like I wanted to feel morally superior to those who only went in the good times. I remember that last game of the season when they had to beat Sheffield and we had to keep an eye on the telly at the back of the stand to see how Castleford were doing. The noise that day, from about 6,000 fans, was incredible. You just cannot believe the noise they can make when there is something to fight for.

Trevor Gibbons

Chartered Plane to Cardiff

I used to help with stoking the braziers, which were placed on the pitch on a frosty night before a big game to make sure the game could be played. We used to get our twopenny tickets from school to watch Hull. Then when I was one of the vice-presidents of the club we chartered a plane to fly down to Cardiff for a match. Hull FC means everything to me, literally. They've broke my heart more times than I care to remember. My wife is always saying 'Oh, here he goes again. He's never going to buy a pass again.' I was so distraught after one match that I ripped my pass up in the bar. I was never ever going to set foot in that bar again. It went round the ground like wildfire. A few days later I bumped into David Latham, who was chairman then, and I told him I would never set foot in The Boulevard again. But he got the club to send me a new pass and I went back. I think the black and white irregular hoops are great but the jersey I did like was

Roy Francis still feels at home in the trainer's hut at The Boulevard although he is pictured as the Leeds coach in 1967, three years after ending a long and successful career at Hull. In front, covered with a blanket against the cold, is former winger Ivor Watts, then Hull's assistant coach.

Graham Bray scores a vital try in the 1980 RL Challenge Cup semi-final defeat of Widnes.

the old black-with-a-white-V one. They won the championship wearing that. Like the Aussie jersey it makes the players look that bit bigger, especially across the shoulders. I thought Hull looked monsters when they wore it. Some of the players today look like dwarfs.

Mike Adamson

Threepenny Stand Lured Aussies

The Threepenny Stand crowd created a terrific atmosphere and I remember when we played Australia in 1982 and nearly beat them it was electric. I know a lot of the Aussie players we signed later, like Peter Sterling, had said one of the reasons they came was because they remembered

the atmosphere of that night. I was in favour of the merger with Gateshead because it would have meant the end for us otherwise. But the big thing is that they called us Hull FC, went back to the irregular black and white hooped jerseys and we stayed at The Boulevard. That was like the Holy Trinity. And *Old Faithful*, of course. As long as they kept them, they could do what they liked with the rest. I write for the fanzine *Any Kind of Weather* and they started a 'Bring back the irregular black and white hoops' campaign, which was picked up by the *Hull Daily Mail*. I do feel that Hull supporters are somehow different from the rest. It could be because we are out on our own as a city. I mean, you have Bradford, Leeds and a few other places close together, but it's Hull and nobody else for miles. When there was that time it looked as if Hull might have to pack up, I was distraught. My wife got quite annoyed with me for being so down about it. But if it had happened it would have been like a bereavement. Next to my family, Hull FC means everything to me. Even my mobile phone plays *Old Faithful* when it rings.

Ian Roberts

Like One Big Family

The atmosphere is still good at The Boulevard. I've started taking my little lad. He's ten and we sit with all these other passholders in the East Stand, Section B. There's about fifty of us who all sit together and have been for about three years. So we all know each other now. It's like a big family and we all have a good laugh. It's great because where we sit, the space to the left of us is reserved for the opposition coaches and we give them some stick. It's all in fun and they mostly take it in good part. We had a right ding-dong with Frank Endacott, the Wigan coach. He's a really good character and we had a right good laugh with him. He came and had a word with us at the end of the game and saw us in the bar afterwards. He's a really funny character. That's the good thing about the game and now I've started taking my little lad, it's nice to see something like that. You know, they see coaches on telly and they seem a bit distant to you at that age. But to see them in the flesh and see that they are good genuine people I think that's good for young kids.

Mike Poole

Passes for Skippers

I remember Rossy Brothers, the bookies. They always had a book full of passes to see Hull play and when trawler skippers came back from fishing, they would pick one up. My Uncle Maurice used to hire a taxi for midweek matches and he'd go as far as Huddersfield to see Hull play. An incident that stands out was when Hull played at Oldham in a Championship play-off match and Tommy Harris smacked Oldham's Pitchford. He stretched him out and walked off. But the referee called him back and said: 'Wait for me to tell you. Now, you're off.' There was another match at Oldham when one of the Drake twins was sent off and they say that when the player he hit went for a bath it was full of blood. It was like that then.

Aubrey Coupland

Hessle Road Families Gone

One of the reasons crowds might be down is because a lot of Hessle Road has been knocked down and at one time you'd get a lot of fans from there. Whole families went. Just take my father's family. There were my uncles Bill, Ted, Brian, Walt and my granddad. They'd all meet in Rosamond Club, have three or four pints and then go to the match. That's what you did in those days. They'd work until twelve o'clock on a Saturday and go straight to the clubs, Dee Street Club, Albert Club, Subway Club or meet in Rayners or Alexander pubs. They'd stay until quarter to three and then go to the match and that's why Threepenny Stand

Hull pulled off a major international signing coup when they captured three of the 1981 New Zealand tour squad. Left to right: Gary Kemble, Dane O'Hara and James Leuluai.

will never burn. Hull has always been a big part of my life. I get withdrawal symptoms at the end of the season. I was off work the other week so I got the videos out and watched Hull beat Wigan in the Cup and a few others.

Bob Cone

Changed My Life

Hull FC means everything to me. It has taken over my life. I'd always been a supporter, going to the games, but never more than that. I was involved in scouts and another youth movement for about eighteen years, which took up a lot of my time. But when I gave it up I decided I wanted to get more involved in Hull FC. So I became a vice-president. But the thing that changed my life really was a chance meeting with Vince Groak, which led to us starting the Hull fanzine. Then we helped form the Hull Independent Supporters' Association and we became the sort of unofficial voice of the fans at the time when the club went through all those problems with David Lloyd and talks of take-overs and mergers. So I'm chairman of HISA, co-editor of the fanzine and a member of the vice-presidents. I never know which hat to wear when I go to The Boulevard. But we have a brilliant relationship with the club now and Hull's chief executive, Shane Richardson, regularly invites us to meetings to tell us what he's doing and asks our opinion. I've always gone in Threepenny Stand. I used to stand at the '25' at the scoreboard end on the rails when I was a kid and then moved my way back up the stand. Then when just that little bit of Threepenny Stand was left, I moved into that. As a vice-president I've got a seat in the best stand, but I transfer the pass for the Threepenny Stand. I tried one season in the best stand seats, but I didn't like it. I've always said that the day I have to sit down to watch a game is the time to chuck it. Apart from anything else I don't think it's a good ground to watch from anywhere else but Threepenny Stand.

Steve Roberts

Trawling for Support

You hear some stories about fanatical Hull supporters that you wonder if they are true. There is one about a Hull fan in the

Patrick Entat, the French Test scrum-half who played a key part in Hull's 1991 Premiership Trophy final victory.

1950s who was a trawlerman. He'd just landed early one morning and he asked someone how Hull had got on in a Cup-tie at home to Workington. He was told they'd drawn. 'When's the replay?' he asked. 'This afternoon', he was told and straight away he hailed a taxi, showed the driver a fistful of pound notes and said 'Take me to Workington'. Hull were very popular among the trawlermen and they would keep in touch with the wireless operator who would pick up the scores. In the old days the Threepenny Stand was filled with fish dock workers and they were always ready with a quick crack. Blackpool Borough once played a Cup-tie at The Boulevard and a few of their supporters came round throwing sticks of rock into the stand. 'Thanks,' said one Hull fan. 'If there's a replay we'll come and throw cod ends at your lot.' I remember a match in the early Fifties when Hull were playing Wigan. Hull were just emerging as a promising team and to have beaten the mighty Wigan would have been quite something. It was a close game and late on a Hull player broke through for what I think would have been a vital or even match-winning try. But he turned back when he heard the whistle only for the referee to say he hadn't blown. It turned out somebody in the crowd had blown the whistle and there was a hell of a rumpus.

Charles Arnold

Little Terry Devonshire is faced by Wigan's mighty Billy Boston in a 1963 RL Challenge Cup-tie.

CHAPTER 7
For the Love of Hull

The family game. Hull's David Maiden (left) and Castleford's Adrian Vowles with wives and children before the teams met in a Super League game.

Hull of a Holiday

The club is the greatest love of my life in sporting terms. It also affects my family life. For instance, I said to my wife a few years ago 'How would you fancy a weekend in The Lake District?' She thought it was a great idea until I said 'Oh, by the way, Hull are at Workington on the Sunday so we could go watch them.' She said 'I might have known.' To make up for it, the next season I promised I would take her to Paris for a weekend. She'd always wanted to go there, but straightaway she said 'And what rugby match will that be, then?' I had to admit it was Hull against Paris St Germain. I'd planned it because Hull had just got promoted to Super League. Then Paris dropped out, so we never did get there. But she knows when we do get away for a weekend during the season it coincides with where Hull are playing. And I can say that I have scored a try and kicked the goal on The Boulevard pitch. It was at midnight after my fiftieth birthday party held in the bar under the Threepenny Stand.

Steve Roberts

Gently Does It

A funny happening at The Boulevard in the Sixties at a Hull *v.* Halifax game was when this old guy finally snapped in frustration with the ref. and got over the small fence in front of the Threepenny Stand and started to approach the referee. Colin Dixon, the Halifax centre, intervened on the ref's behalf. He picked the pensioner up, carried him back to the fence and gently and calmly deposited him

back into the stand to the great amusement and cheering from the crowd. We were once all sat in the Clarendon, our local, when my mate Les said he had a video of *The Life of Brian*, a film which I had not seen as it was banned in Hull by the local council. At this time 'God' was Brian Smith and he was about to return home to Aussie after doing such a fantastic coaching job at The Boulevard. The club had brought out a video of all the highlights of his time with Hull. Now, when Les handed me the video film my other mate, George, grabbed it and said he hadn't seen *The Life of Brian Smith* and took it home. The following Friday he came bursting into the pub swearing and threatening. 'I watched that for an hour and it's nothing about Brian Smith. It's full of Arabs'.

B.J. Knott

Replay for Wedding

I remember we missed a Cup-tie because it was our wedding day, but they drew 10-10 and we were at the replay on the Wednesday night. We were on the coach and everybody was saying 'What the hell are you doing here, why aren't you on your honeymoon?' But we said we can't miss the replay. I think Hull drew the tie for us and then won the replay. It was a good wedding present. On our wedding day my father-in-law was sat there listening to the match on the radio telling us what was going on. I actually got married with one black and one white sock on. My best man had the other black and white socks on.

Andy Scarah

Pigeons Come First

I knew Johnny Whiteley's dad real well because we both raced pigeons. I still do. I also knew Johnny's brother, Peter, and it was in his Buckingham club that we had our Pigeon Federation headquarters. The only times I miss an away match is on a Friday because my pigeons go away on a Friday to race on a Saturday. Years ago, when Hull played on a Saturday, I used to be sat waiting for my pigeons and as soon as I got them in I was on my bike and off to the match. I've even gone in at half-time. I have to admit I put my pigeons first. If I send them to a race then I think they deserve for me to be there when they come back to feed and talk to them. I don't give them Hull players' names. I might lose if I did.

Barry Scarah

Shirt Nicked

When I was in the army in Colchester, the first thing I got for Christmas was a black and white shirt. I only had it a couple of months before somebody nicked it. At least it's good to think there might still be somebody walking round Colchester with a Hull shirt on. The old black and white shirt looked great and I didn't go along with the change and Hull being called the Sharks. I called it the demented fish because that's what it looked like to me. I used to imagine the headlines 'Hull play like right pilchards', so I was glad when they got rid of the Sharks.

Graham Foot

Shareholder at Sixteen

I joined the shareholders when I was only sixteen, which was very young for that sort of thing. I just got the minimum amount of shares, twenty-five, which enabled me to go along to the meetings and see what it was all about. I remember being at a shareholders' meeting when Brian Smith said he had this key Australian player lined up to come over but they didn't have the financial backing to do it. It was as at that point that we started a £1 lottery, which was basically the supporters raising £50,000 to bring Noel Cleal over. It was around then that I also got to know about the West Riding branch of the Hull Supporters' Club. This was a small group of supporters who were living in West Yorkshire and had three or four meetings a season at a Leeds pub. There were about thirty members. We had an end of season player presentation for about ten years and representatives from the club like coach Brian Smith and Aussie scrum-half Peter Sterling came over and seemed to enjoy it. I didn't have a car then, but the West Riding Supporters' Club used to have a network of people who you could phone up and get a lift to matches.

Richard Wilson

Airlie Bird on Honeymoon

I've just been on my honeymoon and I felt proud to wear my Hull shirt on the aeroplane and in Las Vegas, Los Angeles and Hawaii. I take it with me every time I go away. I feel real proud wearing it. I'm surprised they never brought the Airlie Bird nickname back. I mean the mascot they've got now is awful. I've still got a badge from when I went to Wembley as a kid and it's got Airlie Bird on it. I always wake up early in the morning and when we moved into a bungalow a couple of years ago I wanted to put up an Early Bird plaque so that it sort of referred to me getting up early and supporting Hull FC.

Mark Donoghue

Snookered

I remember David Barends playing for Bradford Northern under floodlights at The Boulevard. He was a black winger and the white ball dropped on his head from a high kick. Well, a wag in Threepenny Stand immediately shouted 'White in off black – seven away' Then there was the time during Hull Fair week when the trainer ran on the field with a plastic bag of water and another Threepenny Stander shouted 'Eh mate, have you lost your goldfish?' I remember in the Fifties somebody – I think everybody called him Shep – used to go round the perimeter at The Boulevard with a bike pulling a trailer. He had made up something in black and white that was supposed to be an Airlie Bird. So who says the Rhino mascot and all the others are new?

Eric Gibbons

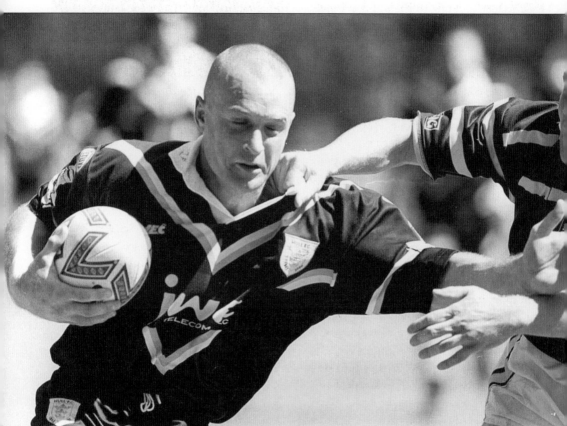

David Maiden, who was one of the Gateshead Thunder squad to move to Hull following the merger.

Great Travelling Days

I will always remember the way we used to travel round the country to every match in the Eighties. A group of us lived in North Yorkshire and Teesside and we used to stop at sleepy little pubs all over the place on the way there and back. We'd totally confuse all the regulars when we went in dressed in our black and white replica shirts. The locals couldn't understand it. We became match day regulars at the Middleton Arms in North Grimston and always used to talk with an old boy called Tommy. He had watched Leeds once and always told us about a player called Deakin. His script never changed: 'He were a good player that Deakin. He had a son who played as well. He was called Deakin, too.' A great trip was to Whitehaven. A minibus-load of us decided to have a weekend away. We stayed in a Penrith hotel on the Saturday night. I had one over the eight, and when I blinked my contact lens fell out. We'd had a few and there were so many people milling about we left it on the floor. There was no chance of finding it. On the Sunday lunch time we went to the Twa Dogs pub in Keswick, arriving just before they opened at twelve o'clock. A few minutes later a full supporters' club coach and a few cars full of Hull FC fans turned up, having arranged to meet us. The landlord was gobsmacked but grateful. I can't remember a lot about the match, except that we won and Whitehaven seemed a bit dark and derelict. I will always remember that group of fans who travelled all over together including The Dong, the twins, Knocker-head, Gasper, Tilly, Bluenose, Crazy Blanket and the rest. During this period we went to every game and there was a weekend when Hull played three games in places like Cumbria and Leigh and we went to them all. Then we joined the

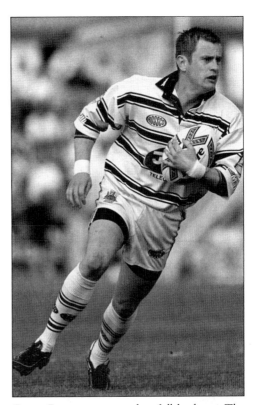

Steve Prescott, a popular full-back at The Boulevard.

West Yorkshire branch of the Hull Supporters Club and there was about twenty or so of us travelling around. Now our memories of that time are almost as much to do with the bunch of people we were with as with the game itself. They were great times. We still see each other at games, but we are now a little more sedate and older.

Rob Lonsdale

One-legged Assault

My dad had just had his leg amputated and he was sat in the best stand at Oldham's Watersheddings. This bloke was giving him a lot off and my dad turned round and decked him even though he only had one leg. So they brought the coppers and my dad hit one of them with his crutch. I remember walking outside and finding my mum in tears. I asked 'What's up?' and she said 'They've arrested your dad, look'. And there he was leaning against the gate because they'd taken the crutches off him until the bus came. I also take Hull getting beat pretty badly. I've come home from a match, rowed with my wife, my tea's gone in the fire and she's walked out because I'm sat there sulking.

Mike Adamson

Lucky Underpants

I'm a very superstitious person and I go through quite a lot of rituals for Hull to win. The season we got promoted into Super League I'd been to every home game except the Featherstone match when we could have clinched the title right at the back end of the season. But they lost and it was the day I flew out to Philadelphia where I was to work for fifteen months. I tried to get it changed but couldn't. So I flew out in my Hull shirt and my lucky socks and underpants on, which my wife subsequently threw away when we got beat. The first thing we did when we got off the plane was to ring my dad and I was gutted when he told me they'd got beat. The elation came a week later when we beat Huddersfield to clinch the title. I found out outside a McDonalds in Philadelphia where I'd rang my dad from a public call-box. The locals must have thought I was mad because I was jumping around and singing *Old Faithful* in the car-park. My dad sent me the video of the game. It cost about thirty quid to get it formatted. He sent quite a few others, so I was still able to follow them from America. Another superstition was my mum was never allowed to wash our scarves if we got on a Cup run. So we invariably turned up at Wembley not looking our best with our black and black scarves. Another one is that I never look when the opposition put a bomb in the air. I listen to the crowd and if I hear the cheering I'll look again. That probably started when I was young and I'll have watched our full-back drop a ball. Though I don't remember doing that when Gary Kemble was there, because I never had any fear of him dropping the ball. And I won't look at the scoreboard, but that's only at The Boulevard. There was also a time when I would go to the toilet if we needed a try because I'd done that once and Hull had scored a vital late try.

Ian Roberts

Dominoes and Pint Before Match

We used to do anything to be involved when we were kids. You know, run errands for them or carry trainer's bucket. I remember once when the chairman came out and asked if anyone knew Dee Street Club. I stepped forward and he said 'Here's threepence, get on your bike and go to Dee Street Club and tell Jimmy Courtney he's playing this afternoon.' Off I went and found Courtney, who was quite a good half-back, playing dominoes in the club with a pint on the table. I told him the chairman wanted him to go and play for Hull. He said to tell him to wait. He then finished his game of dominoes and his pint – and I think he'd already had a few – before setting off for the game. The funny thing is they say he played the game of his life. But they said when you put your head down in that pack you were intoxicated by the breath.

Aubrey Coupland

Dash from Match to Wedding

The day I got married Hull played at St Helens. It should have been played on the Sunday but it was switched to Saturday and Alf Macklin, who was a mate of mine and played on the wing for Hull, came straight from the match at St Helens to my wedding reception at the Polar Bear pub. I remember Hull playing at Manchester United's Old Trafford ground when Huddersfield beat them and at half-time I went for three pints. I was trying to make my way to my seat when this copper said 'You can't do that' and helped me to carry my beer to my seat. You wouldn't get that at a soccer match.

Bob Cone

Souvenir Sawn Off

When Hull played their last game in front of the old Threepenny Stand, I took a hacksaw to the match because I wanted to saw off a bit of wood for a souvenir. After the game finished I waited for the crowd to wander off and I just sat down and started sawing where I would normally stand. I just wanted a little piece. But when I looked up I was surrounded by yellow-coated stewards. The head steward asked me what I was doing and I said: 'Well they're knocking it down tomorrow, they won't want this bit'. But he

said: 'One more saw cut and I'll have you arrested'. There was a copper stood not far away, so I thought discretion was the better part of valour. But I told the steward he was a miserable so and so, before wandering off. Then I went round the end of Threepenny Stand and came back through the middle bit and cut a bit off there instead. I got it varnished and mounted with a little plaque saying what it is. Hull could have made thousands of pounds if they had sold the rest of Threepenny Stand bit by bit.

Steve Roberts

Arthur Keegan, a great and popular full-back in the Fifties and Sixties.

Lee Jackson, back at Hull after playing for Sheffield Eagles, Australia's Newcastle and Leeds Rhinos.

'FC Forever – Merger Never' said the banner as feelings ran high when it was feared a merger with Gateshead Thunder would mean the end of Hull FC. Thankfully, it was not to be.

Epilogue

Listening to so many stories in the process of compiling this book brought back memories of my father telling me about the great Hull team that won the Cup in 1914. The Billy Batten stories must have been exaggerated because from what he told me I thought he must have been about seven feet tall and over twenty stone. I used to smile when he talked about Jack Harrison, who was killed in action and awarded the Victoria Cross in the First World War just after he'd broken the record for most Hull tries in a season. 'Harrison was a good winger,' he'd say, 'But a bit timid!' Like me. The Threepenny Stand crowd has always had a reputation for barracking opposition players and even letting their own players know what they think of them if they are not playing well. I got a small taste of this when I played for Hull Juniors in my first match for them after leaving schoolboy rugby. I was a skinny full back and we were playing a rough house lot from Hull Boys Club. It was a curtain-raiser before one of Hull's big games and the ground was already packed. Early in the game the opposition put up a high kick towards me. I could hear the forwards tearing down on me, including John Taylor, who later signed for Hull KR and went on tour with Great Britain. I chickened out and let the ball bounce. That did it. Threepenny Stand erupted and jeered every time a high kick went near me. Mind you, I remember the great Lewis Jones admitting he never played well at The Boulevard because of the crowd.

Raymond Fletcher

OLD FAITHFUL

Old Faithful is the Hull battle hymn that was first sung by their fans over sixty years ago and is still roared out just as lustily today. The origins are unclear, but the general belief is that the cowboy song became popular nationwide at about the time that Hull won the championship in 1936, and was taken up by their supporters.

The popular version is:

Old Faithful, we'll roam the range together
Old Faithful, in any kind of weather
When your round up days are over
There'll be pastures white with clover*
For you, Old Faithful pal of mine

Giddy up old fella
'Cos the moon is yellow tonight
Giddy up old fella
'Cos the moon is mellow and bright
There's a coyote howling to the moon above
So carry me back to the one I love
Giddy up old fella
'Cos we gotta get home tonight

* An *alternative line often sung by fans is:*
And The Boulevard's white with clover